CORRECTIONS, PEACEMAKING,

AND RESTORATIVE JUSTICE

transforming individuals and institutions

michael braswell
east tennessee state university

john fuller
the state university of west georgia

bo lozoff
the human kindness foundation

anderson publishing co.
2035 Reading Road
Cincinnati, OH 45202
800-582-7295

**Corrections, Peacemaking and Restorative Justice:
Transforming Individuals and Institutions**

Copyright © 2001
Anderson Publishing Co.
2035 Reading Rd.
Cincinnati, OH 45202

Phone 800.582.7295 or 513.421.4142
Web Site www.andersonpublishing.com

Library of Congress Cataloging-in-Publication Data

Braswell, Michael.
    Corrections, peacemaking, and restorative justice : transforming individuals and
institutions / Michael Braswell, John Fuller, Bo Lozoff.
        p.   cm.
    Includes bibliographical references and index.
    ISBN 1-58360-519-3 (pbk.)
    1. Corrections--Philosophy. 2. Criminals--Rehabilitation. 3. Reconciliation.
4. Restorative justice. I. Fuller, John R. II. Lozoff, Bo. III. Title.
HV8665 .B73 2000
364.6--dc21

                                                        00-063970

Cover digital composition and design by Tin Box Studio, Inc.

EDITOR Gail Eccleston
ASSISTANT EDITOR Genevieve McGuire
ACQUISITIONS EDITOR Michael C. Braswell

This book is dedicated to anyone
who needs a second chance.

Acknowledgments

No book is ever completed without the help of friends, family, and colleagues, and this one is no exception. We would like to thank the following graduate students for their assistance and support: Mario, Jaison, Amy, Laura, Chasity, Kim, and a special thanks to Kim Dodson and Buddy Humphries. Special thanks also go to Sharon Elliott for her typing assistance and to our wives, Susan, Amy, and Sita for their support. We are especially indebted to friend and colleague, John Whitehead, who co-authored Chapter 2 and reviewed the entire manuscript, making a number of helpful suggestions. Thanks also go to Morton Brown and Jack Higgs for reading portions of the manuscript and to Jarvis Masters and Padma Publishing for letting us use some of Masters' essays. We highly recommend his book, *Finding Freedom*, which can be ordered from his publisher (Padma Publishing, Junction City, CA). Finally, we are indebted to Anderson Editor Gail Eccleston, whose skill and talent made this a better book.

Michael Braswell
John Fuller
Bo Lozoff

Contents

Part II
DOING PEACEMAKING

If I could sum up my entire education experience and reflection in a single sentence, it would be: Things are not what they seem.
– Hans Mattick

There are two kinds of criminals: those who get caught and the rest of the human race.
– Charles Colson

In the beginner's mind, there are many possibilities. In the expert's, there are few.
– Suzuki Roshi

Chapter 1

Introduction

An Overview

Corrections, in its most rudimentary form, is approximately 300 to 400 years old beginning, for purposes of American Corrections, in eighteenth-century England. The initial era of corrections offered less than humane conditions of incarceration and included corporal and capital punishment as well as exile to first American and then Australian colonies. Mixing men, women, and children together in overcrowded facilities resulted in hunger, rape, and other forms of degradation and violence. These conditions often created an atmosphere of unrelenting despair and depravity. Persons like John Howard (1726-1790), the Quaker, Elizabeth Fry (1780-1845), Captain Alexander Maconochie (1787-1860), Sir Walter Crofton (1815-1897), and John Augustus (1784-1859) made noteworthy efforts to restore a sense of humanity and create hope in the evolution of correctional process.[1] They, and others like them, experienced only limited success, but more importantly, they planted the seeds of hope's possibilities. Such possibilities have been reflected in the more recent rehabilitation, peacemaking, and restorative justice movements.

While corrections is several hundred years old, peacemaking, as reflected in such ancient-wisdom traditions as Christianity, Judaism, Taoism, Hinduism, Buddhism, Islam, and Native American religion, is several thousand years old. Like their correctional counterparts, many of the founders and leaders of these wisdom traditions experienced only limited success during their lifetime, but the seeds they planted have stood the test of time. The influence of these traditions is evident in organized religions, civil rights traditions, contemporary spiritual movements, humanistic psychology, certain types of psychotherapy, peacemaking criminology, and the current restorative justice movement.

This particular book is designed to view peacemaking as a broad, encompassing process that, while grounded in ancient philosophical and spiritual traditions, is expressed in many different shapes and forms; from Nel Nodding's feminist concept of caring to Charles Colson's prison fellowship movement; from the militant nonviolence of Gandhi to Martin Luther King, Jr.'s Baptist version practiced in the Civil Rights Movement of the 1960s; from the Buddha's four noble truths to Mother Teresa's serving and perceiving the poor and dying as "Christ in a distressing disguise"; from sweat lodges being used with incarcerated Native Americans as a part of a spiritual transformation process to Buddhist monks teaching death row inmates how to meditate. Each movement and effort is not simply about understanding peace, but also about becoming more peaceful ourselves through practicing personal awareness and more mindful living wherever we might work and live. Thich Nhat Hanh writes, "Once we learn to touch this peace, we will be healed and transformed. It is not a matter of fact; it is a matter of practice."[2] This book is about personal and institutional transformation. From the one to the many, the process of change starts in the individual human heart. Such change cannot be forced, but comes only through consent.[3] Peacemaking is a natural outgrowth of being at peace, from one's inner life to external expressions and actions that influence one's community and the institutions of society. Joan McDermott suggests that the "personal is also political," and that cultural evils such as poverty, racism, and sexism may create a kind of structural violence that makes personal transformation difficult for those who are oppressed.[4] What she wrote is true and perhaps Charles Dickens famous line, "It was the best of times. It was the worst of times," is appropriate for any age where the structure of culture interacts with the needs and will of the individual. Still, it also seems fair to consider that while we cannot necessarily control what culture or life in general brings us, we do have a choice in how we respond to whatever comes our way. We would suggest that whether one refers to a sense of the sacred in the context of the human spirit or holy spirit, transformed persons who live their lives from the inside-out are more likely to lead to more just and peaceful communities and societies.

Chapters 1 through 3 are designed primarily to provide readers with both philosophical and spiritual context for peacemaking that forms a foundation for understanding the potential for peacemaking in criminological thought, the criminal justice system, and society in general (e.g., community justice). Chapter 2 examines the roots of peacemaking through "compassionate corrections" as inspired by the ancient wisdom traditions of Judaism, Christianity, Islam, Buddhism, Taoism, and Native American spirituality. In Chapter 3, "Peacemaking Criminology" is explored through the work of such criminologists as Richard Quinney and Hal Pepinsky. Beginning with Chapter 4, the focus moves from thinking about peacemaking to doing peacemaking; how one can develop in a spiritual context, a peacemaking attitude and become a force for personal and social peace. Chapter 5 explores how one moves from personal change to influencing institutional change by examining such issues as punishment and treatment and the potential for restoration and reconciliation. Chapters 6 and 7 explore personal commitment to the peacemaking process through Bo Lozoff's correspondence with prisoners for more than 20 years, and through Jarvis Masters' stories about prison life written from his cell on death row at San Quentin. Chapter 8 examines the peacemaking process on a broader, more systemic basis through the current restorative and community justice movement. This chapter attempts to bring peacemaking and corrections back into a focus that integrates personal and institutional transformation and commitment with the informal power of the community to address suffering and restore both victims and offenders.

Understanding and Doing Peacemaking in Context

The context for understanding and doing peacemaking is multi-dimensional and consists of personal, social, and criminal justice domains. Each of these domains has its own unique characteristics and yet overlaps with the other domains. For example, as individuals we do not live and act in a vacuum. If we decide to do something, our actions typically affect others, including family, friends, and other individuals living in our community. If we decide to "legally" cheat a neighbor out of his or her property, our action affects our personal reputation—how others perceive us as being irresponsible and untrustworthy. The context for such an act also includes the social dimension, which results in our undermining the social peace and trust of our neighborhood. When we contribute to social injustice in our community, people are more likely to feel vulnerable to exploitation. Of course, if we commit a crime, such as fraud, in cheating our neighbor out of his or her property, we also diminish the sense of security and confidence persons have who live in our community. In addition, we become a part of national crime statistics and the criminal justice system, which in turn may increase the general fear of Americans concerning being victimized by criminals.

One of the authors has used personal, social, and criminal justice contexts for a number of years as a teaching perspective for his course on "Justice and Ethics." The idea of community, whether one is talking specifically about ethics or more broadly about peacemaking, includes personal views and beliefs interacting with the views and beliefs of others within the legal boundaries of our governing system. These contexts or dimensions are interconnected and interdependent. The idea of community may also include our physical environment—the air we breathe, the land, water, and animals that sustain us as well as our personal, social, and political environments.

When we examine peacemaking, our personal beliefs are called into question. What do we really think about the idea of peacemaking? Does "might make right" or should we look out for the "least of those" in our community, even if they happen to be incarcerated in prisons? Is our peace of mind more important than a piece of the action? What are we willing to sacrifice (in terms of money, status, and success) in order to be at peace and be a peaceful influence in the lives of others?

The social dimension of the peacemaking process includes both direct and indirect interactions between ourselves and others. Do we know our neighbors or prefer to be left alone? Is there a welcome mat at our front door or a "keep out" sign in our front yard? Do we value sharing and relating to those persons who live around us or do we remain suspicious of their motives? Is it only about me or is it also about us? Is every person in it for himself or herself or are we all in it together? The social dimension is not only about how we judge others but also how we judge ourselves in relationship to others. Frederick Buechner writes, "We are all of us judged every day. We are judged by the face that looks back at us from the bathroom mirror. We are judged by the faces of the people we love and by the faces and lives of our children and by our dreams. Each day finds us at the junction of many roads, and we are judged as much by the roads we have not taken as by the roads we have."[5] A colleague commented that the idea and experience of community in the twenty-first century has changed from that of the nineteenth and early twentieth century. In the twenty-first century we interact via e-mail and cell phones. We choose our neighbors by signing up for chat rooms. We choose to live in certain neighborhoods with certain socio-economic groups. We send our children to certain schools. If we attend church, that decision is based upon a variety of factors, many of which are consumer-driven. We build our homes with fenced-in backyards and patios rather than front porches. Sidewalks are largely relics of the past since we are inclined to drive everywhere. The social dimension is one of choice where we interact, but with a very select group of people, excluding many others from such interaction.[6] The rapidly developing communication technologies seem to have simultaneously enhanced and diminished the quality of community life. For some who are disabled or incapacitated, these technologies may help them "reach out and touch someone." For others, the same technologies may become a debilitating convenience—communicating whenever they want to yet remaining anonymous or worse, isolated from the positive and sacrificial possibilities of community life. Given the downside of our contemporary community, the social context can still become a bridge between personal and institutional transformation, a bridge where like-minded persons can initiate a community momentum for change at the highest levels of private and government institutions.

The third dimension comprises the "institutional" context specific to the criminal justice system. There are a variety of institutions in our society including education, mental health, religious, and, for our purposes, legal, which impact on the criminal justice system and process. Criminal justice is primarily driven by legal considerations, while the personal and social contexts rely more on moral views and beliefs. Our criminal justice system sets legal boundaries that govern what we can do to others and what they can do to us. If we are peaceful and our community is at peace, criminal justice remains largely inactive and serves only as a warning to those who might consider harming others. In cases where crime is committed, the criminal justice system attempts to mete out justice and punish the offenders on behalf of the victim and the rest of the community. Peacemaking and restorative justice would include mercy within the equation of justice. The goal of peacemaking and restorative justice would include restoring both the victim and, whenever possible, the offender to the community. A significant theme of this book is that for corrections to have any meaningful and lasting positive effects, both personal and institutional transformation has to occur. First comes an increasing sense of personal awareness, followed by more mindful living.

Personal and Institutional Transformation

Personal awareness includes the realization that life is paradoxical and not always what it seems to be, is sometimes absurd, and yet requires us to make choices nonetheless that carry with them consequences that we may or may not desire or understand. Box 1.1 illustrates an existential model for exploring personal awareness.

Box 1.1

The PACTS Model

1. Paradox: "When things are not what they seem."
2. Absurdity: "When life doesn't add up" or "When life seems out of control."
3. Choosing
   a. Commitment: "Deciding to try to change and persevering in one's efforts."
   b. Noncommitment: "Deciding not to change" or "pretending to change," which is, of course, the same decision.
4. Transcending: "Trying to accept responsibility for where I am, but at the same time, having a vision of where I can be." "Being responsible and hopeful at the same time."
5. Significant Emerging: "Understanding more clearly the costs of the choices I am making and making more meaningful and positive choices."

Source: VanVoorhis, P., Braswell, M., and Lester, D. *Correctional Counseling and Rehabilitation* (Cincinnati, OH: Anderson Publishing Co., 2000), p.12.

Personal awareness also includes a growing sense of "connectedness" of how we are connected to each other and our physical environment in community. We are all connected, one generation to the next, the victim to the offender, and the guard to the inmate. Philosophers as diverse as Lao-Tsu and Plato have advocated that we are not isolated individuals, but rather are connected to each other and our environment.[7] Personal awareness in the sense of connectedness to our physical environment helps us to see earth which sustains us as "Mother Earth" rather than as simply a collection of natural resources to be exploited.

More mindful living creates an opportunity for us to move from thinking and talking about peacemaking to doing it, to becoming engaged in peacemaking. Engaged peacemaking recognizes that personal and social peace come from the inside out. For example, order-keeping focuses on the guilty few, while mindfulness reminds us that while certain persons may guilty of offending, we are all responsible for the larger social context in which the offending takes place. Thomas Merton writes, "You cannot save the world with a system. You cannot have peace without charity."[8] Persons who embody engaged peacemaking create and contribute to peaceful elements in social and governmental institutions which in turn can provide a more peaceful influence in the community at large. Mindful living offers the correctional policymaker and practitioner a transcendent vision, one which clearly sees the current dilemmas of corrections and yet, at the same time, has a dynamic sense of hope and vision for what corrections can become. Mindfulness is essential to peacemaking and incorporates such nonrational virtues as care, compassion, and humility. It should be noted that the virtues of care, compassion, and humility can also be viewed as rational, altruistic choices. The idea of such virtues being examined as nonrational moves them into the realm of the "mysterious," compatible with rational thinking yet also beyond human capacity to define their limits. An article on altruism and the holocaust[9] revealed that a surprising number of German citizens hid Jewish friends at great personal risk for the duration of the war and at the same time, remained anti-semitic regarding the rest of the Jewish population—even to the point of supporting their deportation to concentration camps. Viewing such virtues as care, compassion, and humility in the context of the nonrational is an attempt to maintain a sense of inclusion rather than exclusion and integration rather than separation.

From a growing sense of personal awareness to more mindful living in a social context, the possibilities for a like-minded community to contribute to the criminal justice process in a meaningful way expand and multiply. The theme of care in community justice reminds us that we are all connected and whatever we do to the "least of us," whether prisoners, the homeless, or victims of abuse, we ultimately do to ourselves and our children. Martin Luther King, Jr. once said, "We adopt the means of nonviolence because our end is a community at peace with itself.[10] Such a community struggles to be inclusive rather than selective or exclusive. There are many examples of peacemaking and justice in the community, including the work of the Human Kindness Foundation, and the Prison Fellowship, in teaching citizens and inmates, offenders and victims the practice of peacemaking and community justice. Through such efforts, we increase the opportunity for reconciling the larger community to itself; a community which includes tree-lined neighborhoods of playgrounds and barbecues with the maximum-security neighborhoods of concrete and steel.

Mother Teresa once wrote, "I do not agree with the big way of doing things. To us what matters is the individual."[11] Ultimately, it does come back to the individual; the one who experiences personal transformation and, as a result, engages others in peacemaking activities. And as a community of peace-making individuals reaches out to institutions, its influence is felt in a variety of ways. "From the one to the many, from a feeling to a thought to an act to a visionary attitude. It all starts with the still, small voice, a flicker or a whisper . . . waiting to become incarnate through us in our world, right here and right now."[12]

Questions

1. Why is it important for us to try to understand how personal, social, and institutional dimensions of corrections are connected? How does such understanding relate to moral and legal aspects of the justice and peacemaking process?

2. What do you think about the PACTS model as a way to explore personal awareness? Do these elements apply to institutional as well as personal awareness? Give several examples regarding how they might apply.

3. How has our sense of community changed over the years since the time of our grandparents? How have these changes affected our idea of justice and how we should respond to offenders?

Notes

[1]   Johnson, Herbert and Nancy Travis Wolfe (1996). *History of Criminal Justice*, Second Edition. Cincinnati, OH: Anderson Publishing Co.

      Gesualdi, Louis (1999). "The Work of John Augustus: Peacemaking Criminology." *ACJS Today*, 28(3):1, 3-4.

[2]   Hahn, Thich Nhat (1992). *Touching Peace*. Berkeley, CA: Parallax Press. 1-2.

[3]   Braswell, Michael (1990). *Journey Homeward*. Chicago, IL: Franciscan Herald Press.

      Buechner, Frederick (1976). *Wishful Thinking*. New York NY: Harper and Row.

[4]   McDermott, M. Joan. "From a Peacemaking Perspective, Is Personal Change More Important Than Social Change? No." In John R. Fuller and Eric W. Hickey (eds.) (1999). *Controversial Issues in Criminology*. Boston, MA: Allyn and Bacon.

      Braswell, Michael and Wayne Gillespie. "From a Peacemaking Perspective, Is Personal Change More Important Than Social Change? Yes." In John R. Fuller and Eric W. Hickey (eds.) (1999). *Controversial Issues in Criminology*. Boston, MA: Allyn and Bacon.

[5]   Buechner, Frederick (1976). *Wishful Thinking*. New York, NY: Harper and Row. 48.

[6]   From a conversation with John Whitehead.

[7]   Braswell, Michael, McCarthy, Belinda and Bernard McCarthy (eds.) (1998). *Justice, Crime and Ethics*. Cincinnati, OH: Anderson Publishing Company.

[8]   Quinney, Richard (1988). "Crime, Suffering, and Service: Toward a Criminology of Peacemaking." *The Quest*. Winter Issue:71.

[9]   Tec, Nechama (1995). "Altruism and the Holocaust." *Social Education,* 59(6), pp. 348-353.

[10]   Cohen, Carl (1971). *Civil Disobedience.* New York, NY: Columbia University Press. 40.

[11]   de Bertodano, Teresa de (ed.) (1993). *Daily Readings with Mother Teresa.* London: Fount. 48.

[12]   Braswell. 82.

Part I

Understanding Peacemaking

You don't tell the quality of a Master by the size of his crowds.
— Richard Bach

The hidden harmony is stronger than the visible.
— Heraclitus

The way is not in the sky. The way is in the heart.
— Dhammapada

Chapter 2

Compassionate Corrections: Contributions of Ancient Wisdom Traditions

As we look for ways to reclaim and restore those of us who offend and commit crimes against others of us, it is important that we look backward as well as forward; backward into ancient wisdom traditions that offer us the benefit of thousands of years of a kind of natural human empiricism that moves us toward personal and community transformation. Sam Keen writes, "The great metaphors from all spiritual traditions—grace, liberation, being born again, awakening from illusion—testify that it is possible to transcend the conditioning of my past and do a new thing."[1] For the offender in prison or the offender within each of us, transcending our past and "doing a new thing" creates the possibility of peace and meaning in our and other's lives. Such a notion is hopeful news in an age when a punitive sense of pessimism seems to reign supreme as evidenced by longer prison sentences; fewer treatment, educational, and vocational programs; and correctional budgets strained to the limit for constructing new prisons.

Peacemaking draws from a variety of ancient wisdom and religious traditions including Christianity, Buddhism, Hinduism, Islam, Judaism, and Native American. It is both ironic and unfortunate that the legalistic inclinations of these great traditions have often gone against the grain of their founders' teachings. Their histories have often been written in blood rather than peace. When Jesus, Mohammad, Moses, Buddha, and Krishna leave the stage of temporal existence, heirs to the movement often attempt to organize, proselytize, and legalize a religion around their Masters first and their Master's teachings second. Far too frequently, all who challenge or choose not to accept the official, certified version are demonized. Too often, the Teacher's followers pursue the path of the knight rather than the shepherd; the majesty of the king's court comes to hold more allure than the precarious position of serving as the king's and kingdom's conscience.

An Inquisition or Jihad may come more clearly to preserve the power of the state through expressions of torture and violence than the Master's original intent of liberating the spirit of the people and giving hope to the downtrodden. Yet in spite of all the political maneuverings and manipulations—and all of the violence and unnecessary suffering—somehow the transcendent truths of these ancient traditions find a way to express themselves and offer us conviction, hope, and guidance just when we need it most. Their timeless truths find a voice through servant messengers. The civil disobedience of Gandhi or Martin Luther King, Jr., the service to the poorest of the poor by Mother Teresa, the inspiring poetry of Rumi, the encouragement of the Baal Shem Tov or Thich Nhat Hahn represent countless others who live out peacemaking in ways that can potentially transform persons and institutions. Common to each of these wisdom traditions are three elements: (1) *Communion*: a personal, transforming relationship with God or the Other; (2) *Community*: persons in relationship with others who are also seeking to serve the Truth through service to those who are in need; and (3) *Commitment*: devotion to God and/or the Spirit of truth through compassion and loving-kindness, and dedication to peace within and peace without.

The following sections examine in varying degrees and different ways, elements of peacemaking in a selected group of wisdom traditions. Included in each tradition are one or two examples of peacemakers, along with a brief sampling of some of their teachings.

Christianity

Christians have been debating various doctrines for hundreds of years. Sometimes their debates have been relatively civil, but more often than not, such differences of opinion have been expressed through violence, hatred, and sorrow. Of course, this unfortunate path has also been followed at one time or another by other major religious traditions as well. Fortunately, the beliefs and values that affect peacemaking have been expressed more through practice and service than through intellectual debate and doctrinal strife.

The essential teaching of Christianity concerning peacemaking is that all of us are children of God and therefore we are to love one another. Jesus taught us to pray as children of God (Matthew 6:9). He taught us to love one another as he loves us (John 15:12). In fact, Jesus preached that the two highest commandments summarizing all the other commandments are to love God with all one's heart, mind, and soul and to love one's neighbors (Deut. 6:5; Lev. 19:18). This foundation shows us that we are all brothers and sisters and must treat each other with loving-kindness, dignity, and respect.

In criminal justice, unfortunately, one or more of God's children have harmed other of God's children. Jesus preached forgiveness (Matthew 6:14) and love of one's enemies (Luke 6:27). He rejected the law regarding the stoning of a woman caught in adultery (John 8:1). This doctrine of forgiveness (not only once or twice but seven times 70—that is, never ending) is part of the basis for victim reconciliation in the current restorative justice movement. Victims who are Christians have been taught by their founder to forgive one another, otherwise they will be unable to accept the forgiveness and grace of their heavenly Father (Matthew 6:14-15). The importance of love for one's fellow human beings is voiced by the writer of John who wrote: "If someone says, 'I love God,' and hates his brother, he is a liar; for the one who does not love his brother whom he has seen, cannot love God whom he has not seen (I John 4:20). In other words, loving those persons around us who are visible shows that we also love God who is invisible. In one of his central teaching opportunities, the Sermon on the Mount, Jesus also enjoined his followers to be peacemakers for peacemakers . . . "will be called children of God" (Matthew 5:9). Likewise, he instructed his followers to be merciful and to hunger and thirst for righteousness (Matthew 5:6,7). Martin Luther King, Jr., and Mother Teresa are two good examples of Christian peacemakers.

Martin Luther King, Jr., is an example of a peacemaker who attempted to create an ever-widening circle of persons to bring about peaceful changes in communities and institutions. King was well aware of the difficulties and sacrifice required to be a peacemaker. Robert Coles wrote, "Burnout is a surrender," Dr. Martin Luther King, Jr., once said at a conference in 1964. A lot of us were sitting at a table talking about the subject because we had witnessed it in others and in ourselves. He explained his somewhat startling choice of words this way: "We have just so much strength in us. If we give and give, we have less and less and less—and after a while, at a certain point, we're so weak and worn, we hoist up the flag of surrender. We surrender to the worst side of ourselves, and then we display that to others. We surrender to self-pity and to spite and to morose self-preoccupation. If you want to call it depression or burnout, well, all right. If you want to call it the triumph of sin—when our goodness has been knocked out from under us, well, all right. Whatever we say or think, this is arduous duty, doing this kind of work; to live out one's idealism brings with it hazards."[2] Martin Luther King, Jr., referred to his dedicated support group as the "beloved community."

Gandhi's freedom movement in India, based on love and nonviolence, became an inspiration to King as he attempted to right wrongs and transform the American landscape. In fact, before going to a designated place to participate in a civil rights demonstration that often could be life-threatening, demonstrators signed commitment cards that began with the following four commitments: (1) Meditate daily on the teachings and life of Jesus; (2) Remember always that the nonviolent movement . . . seeks justice and reconciliation, not victory; (3) Walk and talk in the manner of love, for God is love; (4) Pray daily to be used by God in order that all men might be free (Levering in DeBenedetti, 1988). Several months before he was assassinated, King gave a sermon in which he said, "I want you to say that I tried to love and serve humanity. Yes, if you want to say that I was a drum major, say that I was a drum major for justice. Say that I was a drum major for peace. That

I was a drum major for righteousness. And all of the other shallow things will not matter. I won't have any money to leave behind. But I just want to leave a committed life behind."[3]

Mother Teresa once said, "If we have no peace, it is because we have forgotten that we belong to each other."[4] She and her sisters chose to focus their sense of family on the "poorest of the poor." When asked how she could continue day in and day out bathing, feeding, and caring for the sick and dying of Calcutta, she responded that when she served the poor, all she saw was "Christ in a distressing disguise." "Though you hide yourself behind the unattractive disguise of the irritable, the exacting, the unreasonable, may I still recognize you, and say: "Jesus, my patient, how sweet it is to serve you."[5] For Mother Teresa, the poor not only referred to those persons who lacked bread to eat, but also to those who were "poor in spirit," the lonely and outcasts. "Before you go out into the world to serve others, how is your home?"[6] Mother Teresa also believed in sacrificial commitment. Being a peacemaker should cost us something. To experience the joy of generosity, we as individuals, need to give "until it hurts." Individual to individual, one person at a time is the way to peacemaking; not the implementation of a peacemaking system from the top down, but doing it door to door, person to person, to whoever is in need that you or I come in contact with . . . Mother Teresa once said, "I do not agree with the big way of doing things. To us what matters is an individual. To get to love the person we must come into close contact with him. If we wait till we get the numbers, then we will be lost in the numbers. And we will never be able to show that love and respect for the person. I believe in person to person; every person is Christ for me, and since there is only one Jesus, that person is the only person in the world for me at that moment."[7] Humility was a cornerstone for Mother Teresa's life. In Box 2.1 are her suggestions for ways we can practice humility.

Box 2.1

> Speak as little as possible of oneself
> Mind one's own business.
> Avoid curiosity.
> Do not want to manage other people's affairs.
> Accept contradiction and correction cheerfully
> Pass over the mistakes of others.
> Accept blame when innocent.
> Yield to the will of others.
> Accept insults and injuries.
> Accept being slighted, forgotten, and disliked.
> Be kind and gentle even under provocation.
> Do not seek to be specially loved and admired.
> Never stand on one's dignity.
> Yield in discussion even though one is right.
> Choose always the hardest.
>
> (de Bertodano:116)

Judaism

A central part of Judaism and in fact the whole Judaeo-Christian tradition is the Ten Commandments (Deuteronomy 4:6-21). Besides enjoining worship of the one God, Yahweh, and no other gods, the Decalogue establishes basic boundaries for human conduct and interaction. Believers are to honor their parents, not kill, not commit adultery, not steal, not bear false witness, and not covet their neighbor's wife or possessions. As at least minimum standards, peacemaking proponents would certainly endorse these rules.

For the covenant Jew, the study of the Torah was one of the most important acts of piety and was regarded as a primary means to protect oneself from evil impulses and acts. To live a moral life, Jews were required to follow God's way in clothing the naked, feeding the hungry, helping the needy, revering parents and teachers, supporting the community, and demonstrating loving-kindness (See Psalm 15).

Hasidism, a mystical movement within Judaism, encourages a more personal and transcendent peacemaking perspective. Communion with God and redemption is found within the inner spiritual life of each person. Hasidism, like other mystical traditions, recognizes that ". . . reality as seen by our eyes cannot be changed, therefore change the eyes which see reality."[8] In many ways, Hasidic Masters defy definition. While they may adhere to rabbinic law in their daily lives, their theological beliefs and expressions often represent polar opposites—from intellectual discourse to inspired outbursts of emotional abandonment. Hasidic parables and stories, and melodies illustrate the presence of God in all aspects of nature and life.

A noteworthy example of peacemaking within the Hasidic tradition is Rabbi Israel who later became known as The Baal Shem Tov (Master of the Name). With the help of his wife, whom he revered as a saint, The Baal Shem Tov embarked upon a journey of developing his inner spiritual life and expressing it outwardly through teaching and helping others, including a group of devoted disciples. The Baal Shem Tov once said, "Before his passing, my father instructed me in these words: 'My son, be sure to remember always that God is with you! Do not ever allow your mind to digress from this awareness' . . . These words were carefully treasured in my heart, and it became my deliberate practice to strengthen within myself the holy conviction that 'the whole earth is filled with God's glory' and that He is really with me at every step."[9]

The Baal Shem Tov's teachings and life could be considered preparation for a life dedicated to peacemaking. They include five major categories. The first is that "God is omnipresent." We need to be aware and pay attention to the "holy sparks" that are found in every aspect of creation. The second category is "Intensive Worship." Becoming aware of God's omnipresence leads one to intensive worship, a longing to experience communion with God. Of course, people are not perfect and mistakes will be made, but according to The Baal Shem Tov, "No one has fallen so low as to be unable to raise himself to God.[10] He reminded his followers, "Man is where his mind is! . . . Forgetfulness of God is exile, remembrance is Redemption."[11] The practice of prayer, meditation, and spiritual study is the way to come to know God. The third and fourth categories are "Help of a Teacher" and "Removal of Obstacles" which are designed to help the devotees become conscious of God in their daily lives. As a teacher, The Baal Shem Tov emphasized the importance of the individual, internal values, specific techniques for practice, redemption and hope, and the heart more than the head. "It is told that when a perplexed father came seeking some light on how to handle his son who was not responding to lecturing and disciplines, this exemplar-teacher simply and characteristically advised, 'Love him more.'"[12] "Interhuman Relations" is the fifth category of The Baal Shem Tov's teachings. He did not judge others. He had a high regard for common people and insisted that one cannot love God if he or she does not love their neighbor.

A Sampling of Hasidic Teachings

The Baal Shem Tov and other Hasidic Masters are known for their stories and parables. These timeless teachings illustrate the power of peacemaking in a variety of ways. The following is a selected sample:

The Baal Shem Tov considered it an art and virtue to listen to others. One day he saw a man who had too much to drink; he was stammering and singing sad songs. The Baal Shem Tov listened attentively, and remarked: "When a man confesses himself, the way he chooses to do it doesn't matter. One may not turn away."[13]

He warned people to be suspicious of anyone claiming to have all the answers: "You want to know if a particular Rebbe is genuine? Ask him if he knows a way to chase impure thoughts from your mind; if he says yes, you'll know he is a fake."[14]

One of Rebbe Mikhal's prayers: "I have but one request. May I never use my reason against truth."[15]

Rebbe Bunim of Pshiske said: "Know that there is more than one path leading to God, but that the surest goes through joy and not through tears. God is not that complicated; He is not jealous of your happiness nor of the kindness you show to others. The road to God goes through man. The sleeping child, the mother caressing him, the old man listening to the rustling of the leaves: God is close to each of them, in each of them God is present."[16]

Rabbi Rafael: "It is a curse when a man measures his behavior to his fellow-men. It is as if he were always manipulating weights and measures."[17]

During a period when the cost of living was very high, Rabbi Mendel noticed that the many needy people who were his guests received smaller loaves than before. He gave orders to make the loaves larger than before, since loaves were intended to adjust to hunger and not to the price.[18]

The Hasidic masters tell the story of the Rabbi who disappeared every Shabat Eve, "to commune with God in the forest," or so his congregation thought. So one Sabbath night they requested one of their cantors to follow the Rabbi and observe the holy encounter. Deeper and deeper into the woods the Rabbi went until he came to the small cottage of an old Gentile woman, sick to death and crippled into a painful posture. Once there, the Rabbi cooked for her and carried her firewood and swept her floor. Then when the chores were finished, he returned immediately to his little house next to the synagogue.

Back in the village, the people demanded of the one they'd sent to follow him, "Did our Rabbi go up to heaven as we thought?" "Oh, no," the cantor answered after a thoughtful pause, "our Rabbi went much, much higher than that."[19]

An old Rabbi once asked his pupils how they could tell when the night had ended and the day had begun.

"Could it be," asked one of the students, "when you can see an animal in the distance and tell whether it's a sheep or a dog?"

"No," answered the Rabbi.

Another asked, "Is it when you can look at a tree in the distance and tell whether it's a fig tree or a peach tree?"

"No," answered the Rabbi.

"Then what is it?" the pupils demanded.

"It is when you can look on the face of any man or woman and see that it is your brother or sister. Because if you cannot see this, it is still night."[20]

Native American

Native Americans offer us the wisdom of the Great Mystery's expression through nature which includes all living things in relationship with each other and the primary elements of life—the sun, rain, wind, fire, and seasons. They considered human beings to be of two minds, the spiritual (higher order) and physical (lower order). The past, present, and future are connected in a seamless mosaic of nature's flow. Chief Seattle in a speech to the governor of the Washington territory in 1854, said, "Every part of this soil is sacred in the estimation of my people. The very dust upon which you now stand responds more lovingly to their footsteps than to yours, because it is rich with the blood of their ancestors, and our bare feet are conscious of their sympathetic touch. For the dead are not powerless. Dead, did I say? There is no death, only a change of worlds."[21]

Paying attention to nature is a Native-American expression of mindfulness. Black Elk reminds us that even the smallest "crawling creature" may have an important lesson to teach us.[22] A part of the sacred tradition of the Hopi Tribe includes a holy woman who is referred to as Spider Woman, a kind of Divine Mother. Edward Hays writes, "like the spider, we must return again and again to rebuild our webs by bringing together the threads of our lives and uniting them to the divine center within. Without such work, our lives become disconnected, unpeaceful and broken."[23] Chief Seattle in another speech also uses the theme of the web: "This we know: the earth does not belong to man, man belongs to the earth. All things are connected like the blood that unites us all. Man did not weave the web of life, he is merely a strand in it. Whatever he does to the web, he does to himself."[24] Black Elk extends this theme of connectedness and peacemaking as it evolves from the one to the many: "The first peace, which is the most important, is that which comes within the souls of men when they realize their relationship, their oneness, with the universe and all its powers, and when they realize that at the center of the universe dwells Wakan-Tanka, and that this center is really everywhere, it is within each of us. This is the real Peace, and the others are but reflections of this. The second peace is that which is made between two individuals, and the third is that which is made between two nations. But above all you should understand that there can never be peace between nations until there is first known that true peace which, as I have often said, is within the souls of men."[25]

Native-American wisdom offers our fast food high-speed modern life a spiritual speed bump. Our rush to buy air and water filters for our homes that are well-equipped with "soothing sounds of nature" CDs, and aroma therapy machines, belies a cynicism and hopelessness whereby we attempt to artificially recreate a connection to nature that we are simultaneously destroying. The speed bump tells us to slow down and pay attention; to re-experience a reverence for the sacrifices required for the food we eat; to recommit ourselves to restoring a harmonious balance with Nature which nurtures us through the air we breathe, the water we drink, and the sun that grows us and our food. The following Ute prayer demonstrates the importance Native Americans place on being connected to Nature as a way to meaning, purpose, and peacefulness in life:

> Earth teach me stillness
>   as the grasses are stilled with light.
> Earth teach me suffering
>   as old stones suffer with memory.
> Earth teach me humility
>   as blossoms are humble with beginning.
> Earth teach me caring
>   as the mother who secures her young.
> Earth teach me courage
>   as the tree which stands all alone.
> Earth teach me limitation as the ant which crawls on the ground.
> Earth teach me freedom
>   as the eagle which soars in the sky.
> Earth teach me resignation
>   as the leaves which die in the fall.
> Earth teach me regeneration as the seed which rises in the spring.
> Earth teach me to forget myself as melted snow forgets its life.
> Earth teach me to remember kindness as dry fields weep with rain.
>   (Brussat & Brussat:162-163)

Buddhism

An Indian Prince, Siddhartha, went on a journey to find the solution to suffering.

Through meditation, he found the solution and became known as the Buddha, the Enlightened One.

Buddha believed and taught that "intuitive wisdom" could lead one to see things as they really are. A primary way he taught was through explaining the Four Noble Truths. One, "all existence is suffering" in the sense that all worldly life is ultimately unfulfilling which is brought on by such desires as fame, sensual pleasures, and power. Two, the cause of suffering is attachment or clinging to that which is impermanent such as desire for fame, sensual pleasures, and power. Third, the cessation of suffering comes from a state of being beyond suffering, which is nirvana. Wei Wu Wei writes:

> Why are you unhappy?
> Because 99.9 per cent
> Of everything you think
> And of everything you do,
> Is for yourself-And there isn't one.[26]

Fourth, the Buddha taught that the Eight-Fold Path is the way one moves toward Nirvana. There is only the universal self. When one becomes aware of this unity, liberation or nirvana occurs. The Buddha believed human beings' attachment to a sense of self or soul led to egoism and selfishness, which resulted in endless desires. In order to be at peace in a transitory life of suffering and sorrow, we must abandon our desires.[27] Non-attachment is not the same as noninvolvement. Rather, through non-attachment one can be more fully and intimately involved in life. In understanding that "what time brings, time takes away," we can learn to let go of our preconceptions and see the unfolding of our lives more clearly. Grasping less and giving more, we can experience that it is indeed "more blessed to give than to receive."

We can see that the experience of non-attachment to what most of us in the West, including offenders and non-offenders, value—possessions, success, fame—could be a basis for peacemaking as demonstrated in the story of the monk who chided a burglar, not for taking the monk's possessions but for not being grateful for them.[28] Such a sense of gratitude and compassion can also be translated into the practice of criminology and criminal justice. Richard Quinney writes, "When we engage in a mean-minded criminology—a criminology of prejudice and punishment—we become the lives that we lead . . . What is required in our work as criminologists, is not only an academic literature and a professional organization, but ways of thinking, speaking, and writing that foster peace. This is a compassionate criminology, a criminology of peacemaking."[29] Because of his Buddhist beliefs, Jarvis Masters, a prisoner at San Quentin, put himself between an intended victim and the prisoner who was planning to kill the person in question. He accomplished this simply by asking the gay inmate for a cigarette. In a sense, Jarvis was less attached to his fear of danger and what others thought of him and saw that the gay prisoner "was just as human as the rest of us."[30]

In our contemporary world, what remains of Buddha and his teachings? "In all Buddhism there remains a trace of his wonderful self-abandonment, of the life that lets itself be wafted into eternity. There remains the Buddhist love which partakes in the suffering and the joy of all living beings and refrains from violence. Despite all the terrible things that have happened in Asia as well as everywhere else, an aura of gentleness lies over the peoples that have been touched by Buddhism. Buddhism is the one world religion that has known no violence, no persecution of heretics, no inquisitions, no witch trials, no crusades."[31]

The Vietnamese monk, Thich Nhat Hanh, is a good example of a contemporary Buddhist peacemaker—as are others, such as the Dalai Lama. The nonviolent and compassionate nature of Buddhists has often resulted in their own persecution and death as recounted by Thich Nhat Hanh during his and fellow monk's experiences during the Vietnam war. Since he and the other monks helped whoever was in need, neither side in the conflict trusted them. As a result, they were often persecuted and killed by both sides. Thich Nhat Hanh notes that mindfulness is a key element in dealing with anger:

> When we are angry, we are the anger. When anger is born in us, we can be aware that anger is an energy in us, and we can accept that energy in order to transform it into another kind of an energy in us, and we can accept that energy in order to transform it into another kind of energy."[32]

Thich Nhat Hanh also reminds us that understanding others as much as possible will help us with our own anger. The person who cuts us off in traffic or is rude at the store is behaving that way for a reason. He or she may be sick or worried about some problem. If we knew where his or her anger came from, we would understand and be less likely to be angry in turn:

> When you understand, you cannot help but love. To develop understanding, you have to practice looking at all living beings with the eyes of compassion. When you understand, you cannot help but love.[33]

Hinduism

Hinduism offers a particular world view. Central to this world view are the concepts of reincarnation (rebirth-redeath): karma, and samsara. The individual soul keeps going through time, keeps dying and being born again, in varying life circumstances. These circumstances depend on "the merit or demerit of the actions (karma) that have taken place in previous forms of existence."[34] Essentially all creatures, all beings, are in the cycle of birth and death. "This is the concept of samsara, the cyclical process that applies to the cosmos and all entities within the cosmos."[35] Within this framework, there are considered to be three ways of seeking salvation: the way of action, the way of knowledge, and way of the love of God.

Perhaps the best-known example of peacemaking in India from the perspective of the West is Mohandas Gandhi, who was to become an inspirational example for Martin Luther King, Jr.

Gandhi was a beloved twentieth-century Indian leader known for his social, religious, and political activism as well as his instrumental role in India gaining independence from England. Born and raised in a privileged caste, he was educated as a lawyer in England. Gandhi's experiences of prejudice in South Africa resulted in him spending 21 years there perfecting a spiritual and political technique he referred to as "truth force." His struggle for Indian self-rule was successful, but it is a sad irony that he was assassinated by a radical Hindu in 1947. Like many other peacemakers who came before and after him, Gandhi was more committed to serving the truth than preserving his own life.

Gandhi's efforts were based on three principles: satya, ahimsa, and tapas. Satya teaches that for one seeking the truth, truth is an intentional lifestyle. Ahimsa focuses on "non-injury" in the active sense—being compassionate to others, even willing to sacrifice one's self for their well-being. Tapas embodies self-restraint in the service of nonviolence and truth.[36] Gandhi once said, "If you love peace, then hate injustice, hate tyranny, hate greed—But hate these things inside yourself, not in another."[37] A powerful illustration of Gandhi's "truth force" involves the story of a distraught Hindu who had been a member of a raiding party that had killed all the Muslims who lived in a particular village except for a small boy. While the hatred between Hindu and Muslim was great, after the killing was over no one knew what to do with the surviving Muslim child.

Who would take care of him? How would he survive? The Hindu man felt great guilt and an overwhelming burden. He sought Gandhi's counsel. After telling his story, Gandhi told him to do two things: (1) raise the child as his own; and (2) raise him as a Muslim. What better way to reconcile the prejudice and hatred one feels for a competing religion than with the love and compassion one feels for one's own child?

The followers of Kabir refuse to acknowledge the caste system, attempt to see God in all people, and recognize that there is only one God who may go by many names. Kabir was born the son of a Moslem, but was a student of the Hindu, Ramananda. Kabir considered himself a child of Rama and Allah, much to the consternation of both Hindu and Moslem clerics. A weaver by trade, Kabir spent his entire life challenging the prejudices of both sides, decrying violence, and proclaiming the love of God. He believed meditation was more important than reading and studying religious traditions.

The poor and disenfranchised flocked to his message of equality, accessibility, and devotion to God. The religious authorities finally banished Kabir and his band of disciples from his hometown. While in exile, he continued to sing and preach the love of God until his death in 1518. "He did not make pilgrimages, he did not practice austerity or celibacy, he did not study. His one spiritual discipline was loving God with all his heart. He was not Hindu; he was not a Moslem; he belonged to both, and to all."[38]

A Sampling of Kabir

He who is brave, never forsakes the battle: he who flies
     from it is no true fighter.
In the field of this body a great war goes forward,
     against passion, anger, pride and greed:
It is the kingdom of truth, contentment and purity,
     that this battle is raging; and the sword that rings forth
     most loudly is the sword of His Name. . . .
It is a hard fight and a weary one, this fight of the truth-seeker:
     for the vow of the truth-seeker is more hard than that of the
     warrior . . .
For the warrior fights for a few hours . . .
But the truth-seeker's battle goes on day and night,
     as long as life lasts it never ceases.[39]

I am neither pious nor ungodly,
I live neither by law nor by sense,
I am neither a speaker nor hearer,
I am neither a servant nor master,
I am neither bond nor free,
I am neither detached nor attached.
I am far from none: I am near to none.
I shall go neither to hell nor to heaven.
I do all works; yet I am apart from all works.
Few comprehend my meaning; he who can comprehend it,
     he sits unmoved.
Kabir seeks neither to establish nor to destroy.[40]

Islam

Islam's holy book, the Qur'an, contains broad directives more than detailed rules for right living. It condemns female infanticide, exploiting the poor, usury, murder, false contracts, adultery, and theft.[41]

The five pillars of Islam are daily prayer, fasting during Ramadan, making a pilgrimage to the holy city of Mecca at least once during one's lifetime, almsgiving, and a profession of faith in the one God and his prophet,

Muhammad. The fourth pillar, almsgiving (zakat), may have the most relevance to peacemaking. This directive is more than just a perfunctory act of portioning out money. It is "a means of redressing economic inequalities through payment of an alms tax or poor tithe. It is an act both of worship or thanksgiving to God and of service to the community. All adult Muslims who are able to do so are obliged to pay a wealth tax annually. It is a tithe or percentage (usually 2.5%) of their accumulated wealth and assets, not just their income. . . . The Qur'an (9:60) and Islamic law stipulate that alms are to be used to support the poor, orphans, and widows, to free slaves and debtors, and to assist in the spread of Islam."[42]

Based on this and other Islamic teachings, Esposito argues that a central thrust of modem Islam is the goal of fostering "an economic development that avoids the excesses of materialism by remaining attentive to the requirements of social justice."[43] This emphasis on social justice is a key aspect of peacemaking. It must also be noted that Islam as well as other wisdom traditions may also be in conflict with contemporary peacemaking philosophies with their emphasis on the masculine and patriarchal framework. "The feminist model would advocate the development of human potential without regard to sex and reject the idea that power is the path to fulfillment.[44] Islamics and conservative Christians would consider that Western society in general and feminists in particular are misguided. They believe that men and women have distinct but complementary roles.

Another potential problem with Islam concerning peacemaking is the concept of jihad or "holy war." If the concept of jihad is limited to the spiritual context of "the constant war which every Muslim must wage against the evil and disruptive tendencies within himself,[45] there is no problem. Even Christians have a long history of noting an individual's "war" with evil, often personified as a war with Satan. Whether Islamic or Christian, if such notions are expressed concretely and used to justify war, terrorism, and inquisitions, then such teachings are obviously incompatible with peacemaking.

Sufism is a mystical movement within Islam that seeks deeper knowledge or experience of God. Rumi, a revered Sufi mystic who was both teacher and poet, embodies the characteristics (compassion, inclusion, service to others, and devotion to God) that mystics from other wisdom traditions also possess. Rumi inspired the Sufi order known as the "Whirling Dervishes."

A Sampling of Rumi's Teachings

"Not for a single moment can you sit inactive, without some evil or goodness issuing from you."[46]

"How should a friend run away from pain inflicted by his friend? Pain is the kernel; friendship is only the husk to it. The sign of true friendship is joy in affliction, calamity, and suffering. A friend is as gold, and affliction is like the fire; pure gold rejoices in the heart of the fire."[47]

"Whenever the self-opinionated man sees a sin committed by another, a fire blazes up in him straight out of Hell; he calls that pride the defense of the faith, not seeing in himself that spirit of arrogance. But defense of the faith has a different token, for out of that fire a whole world becomes free."[48]

"You are so weak. Give up to grace. The ocean takes care of each wave til it gets to shore. You need more help than you know."[49]

"If you want what visible reality can give, you're an employee. If you want the unseen world, you're not living your truth. Both wishes are foolish, but you'll be forgiven for forgetting that what you really want is love's confusing joy."[50]

"Lo, I am with you always, means when you look for God, God is in the look of your eyes, in the thought of looking, nearer to you than your self, or things that have happened to you. There's no need to go outside. Be melting snow. Wash yourself of yourself."[51]

"If you are here unfaithfully with us, you're causing terrible damage. If you've opened your loving to God's love, you're helping people you don't know and have never seen."[52]

"Come, come, whoever you are, Wanderer, worshiper, lover of leaving-it doesn't matter, Ours is not a caravan of despair. Come, even if you have broken your vow a hundred times Come, come again, come."[53]

The Heart of Peacemaking

It is interesting that Islam, Judaism, and Christianity are all concerned with the excesses of materialism while Buddhism, Hinduism, and Native American traditions appear to be largely non-materialistic. Perhaps even more interesting is that the Mystics from each tradition seem to be experiencing and talking about the same thing; the idea that life is always in transition, that things are often not what they seem, that it is essential to love God and serve the truth. As Buechner notes, peace is not happiness—it is not about "the absence of struggle but the presence of love."[54]

The great wisdom traditions all teach that the meaning of life is not found in what we possess, but the kind of person we are. Whether we are literally incarcerated in a prison or not, most of us at one time or another find ourselves hostage through fear and anger to an "inner prison." The wisdom traditions teach us that the way to liberation is through love, compassion, and peace while the way to remaining in our inner prison is through attachment to such things as accumulation of wealth, the attainment of success, and the grasping for power. More importantly, those persons who live out the message of these traditions—Jesus, Buddha, Mohammad, Mother Teresa, Gandhi, and others—show by their lives that the way to peace is difficult but simple, inviting but not compelling. They show us that love, kindness, peace, humility, and determination are much more valuable than financial wealth, estates, or prestige. Such a vision also requires service and sacrifice, and is not without risks. It is no accident that there is also a sense of the prophetic with the ancient Masters. Their teachings stood in contrast to the excesses and corruption of the Kings and Queens of their age. Many of them were martyred as they served as the conscience to the conventional wisdom and traditions of the Institutions of their time.

The way to a deeper peace and happiness is a way we have known for many years, perhaps most of our lives. Yet, we have often chosen to abandon or resist the way to peace for the fleeting promises of the world—our 15 minutes of fame (or in some cases, infamy); the appearance of perfection rather than the contentment of completion. Peace and love and happiness do not exist in some reconstructed sense of social utopia but within ourselves; from the inside out, one day at a time, one person at a time. Moving from peaceful individuals to a peacemaking community which restores the worst of us to the best of us, is a vision worth seeking.

Questions

1. Which of the traditions did you like? Which ones did you not find as appealing? Explain.

2. What do the religious and wisdom traditions explored in this chapter have in common? How are they different?

3. Is "the meaning of life found in what we possess or the kind of person we are?" Would the conventional wisdom of modern society agree or disagree with this quote? Why?

Notes

[1] Brussat, Fredric and Brussat, Mary A. (eds.) (1996). *Spiritual Literacy.* New York, NY: Scribner, p. 434.

[2] Brussat and Brussat, p. 346.

[3] Levering, Ralph B. in Debenedetti, Charies (ed.) (1988). *Peace Heroes*. Bloomington, IN: Indiana University Press, p. 222.

[4] Brussat and Brusatt, p. 349.

[5] de Bertodano, Teresa (ed.) (1993). *Daily Readings with Mother Teresa.* London: Fount, p. 125.

[6] Brussat and Brussat, p. 448.

[7] de Bertodano, p. 48.

[8] Crim, Keith (ed.) (1989). *The Perennial Dictionary of World Religions.* San Francisco, CA: Harper Collins, p. 296.

[9] Berry, Ray (ed.) (1992). *The Spiritual Athlete.* Olena, CA: Joshua Press, p. 83.

[10]   Berry, p. 84.

[11]   Berry, p. 85.

[12]   Berry, p. 86.

[13]   Berry, pp. 87-88.

[14]   Berry, p. 88.

[15]   Berry, p. 89.

[16]   Berry, p. 90.

[17]   Berry, p. 91.

[18]   Berry, p. 92.

[19]   Brussat and Brussat, p. 343.

[20]   Brussat and Brussat, p. 406.

[21]   Brussat and Brussat, pp. 406-407.

[22]   Brussat and Brussat, p. 167.

[23]   Brussat and Brussat, p. 175.

[24]   Braswell, M., McCarthy, B. and McCarthy, B. (eds.) (1998). *Justice, Crime and Ethics.* Cincinnati, OH: Anderson Publishing Co., p. 38.

[25]   Berry, p. 166.

[26]   Wei Wu Wei (1963). *Ask the Awakened.* London: Routledge and Kegan Paul, p. 1.

[27]   Kung, H., van Ess, J., von Stietencron, H. and Bechert, H. (1989). *Christianity and World Religions.* Garden City, NY: Doubleday, 1986.

[28]   Braswell, McCarthy and McCarthy, 1998.

[29]   Quinney, Richard, "A Life of Crime: Criminology and Public Policy as Peacemaking," *Journal of Crime and Justice*, 16:4.

[30]   Masters, Jarvis (1997). *Finding Freedom.* Junction City, CA: Padma Publishers.

[31]   Jaspers, K. (1957). *Socrates, Buddha, Confucius, Jesus: The Paradigmatic Individuals.* York, NY: Harcourt, Brace, and World, p. 39.

[32]   Hanh, Thich Naht (1992). *Peace Is Every Step.* New York, NY: Bantam Books, p. 31.

[33]   Hanh, pp. 79-80.

[34]   Ashby, P.H. p. 308

[35]   Ashby, p. 308.

[36]   Crim, p. 272.

[37]   Brussat and Brussat, p. 348.

[38]   Berry, p. 100.

[39]   Berry, p. 102.

[40]   Berry, p. 109.

[41]   Esposito, John L. (1991). *Islam: The Straight Path.* New York, NY: Oxford University Press.

[42]   Esposito, pp. 90-91.

[43]   Esposito, p. 218.

[44]   Fuller, John, *Criminal Justice: A Peacemaking Perspective.* Boston, MA: Allyn and Bacon, 1998, p. 46.

[45]   Nasr, S.H. (1994). *Deals and Realities of Islam.* San Francisco, CA: Aquarian Press, p. 111.

[46]   Lorie, Peter and Mascetti, Manuela D., (1996). *The Quotable Spirit.* New York, NY: MacMillan, p. 20.

[47]   Lorie and Mascetti, p. 120.

[48]   Lorie and Mascetti, p. 228.

[49]   Brussat and Brussat, p. 182.

[50]   Brussat and Brussat, p. 497.

[51]   Mitchell, Stephen (1989). *The Enlightened Heart.* New York, NY: Harper and Row, p. 54.

[52]   Mitchell, p. 56.

[53]   Safransky, Sy (1990). *Sunbeams.* Berkeley, CA: North Atlantic Cooks, p. 67.

[54]   Buechner, Frederick (1973). *Wishful Thinking.* New York, NY: Harper & Row, p. 69.

The empiricist . . . thinks he believes only what he sees,
but is much better at believing than seeing.
– George Santayana

First-rate intelluctual work requires fresh and iconoclastic thought. . . .
What, after all, is going on here? Where does the truth lie?
– Gilbert Geis

Rather than attempting to create a good society first, and then trying to
make ourselves better human beings, we have to work on the two
simultaneously. The inner and outer are the same.
– Richard Quinney

Chapter 3

Peacemaking Criminology

In Chapter 2, we covered the way major wisdom traditions and religions of the world have incorporated the principles of peace, love, and social justice into their messages. The peacemaking perspective is first and foremost a personal philosophy that starts in the heart of the individual. This chapter, however, extends the peacemaking perspective beyond the individual to the institutional and the cultural context. It is argued that for the peacemaking perspective to be effective, we need an overarching philosophy that allows individual goodness and integrity to be carried on in collective actions, and gives us hope that our institutions and society can be transformed and come to a point of more effectively addressing the problems of crime, the criminal justice system, and corrections. The individual is the necessary starting point. Personal change, however, must lead to social and institutional transformation to achieve our goals of peace and social justice.

Fortunately, we do not have to fashion institutional and societal change from a vacuum. There is a rich history of attempts to induce social change at all levels of society. In this chapter, we will review some of these ideas and theories and suggest how they relate to the peacemaking perspective, particularly as it applies to corrections. Central to our investigation here is the efforts of feminists and critical theorists who have addressed the problems of crime and social justice. By adding these two types of voices to that of the individual transformation outlined in Chapter 2, we hope to show how the peacemaking perspective has a long, diverse, rich, and productive tradition, and that peacemaking can be a lens through which the corrections system can be viewed in a new light. The religious and humanist, feminist, and conflict traditions need not be viewed in isolation from each other. There are scholars and practitioners who incorporate more than one of these traditions and would feel constrained if we were to label them as subscribing to only one tradition. Nevertheless, for our purposes here, it is useful to consider how each contributes to the peacemaking perspective.

Feminist Traditions

At first glance it may seem presumptuous for three men to discuss feminism. We take this step without trepidation, however, because we believe to be fully human is to include the feminist perspective. Feminism is not an ascribed status available only to females. Feminism is a philosophy that argues that men and women should be politically, economically, and socially equal. While many men have not embraced this idea because it challenges their source of dominance, other men have come to recognize that, not only is feminism a fairer way to distribute rewards and opportunities, but that in a patriarchal society, there are costs to men as well as women. The costs of patriarchy to women are, obviously, much more extensive and severe than those to men, and we do not want to deny the oppression of women, but such a way of organizing society is harmful to everyone. Men live shorter lives, are susceptible to more stress, are alienated from their families, and are living lives made dysfunctional by the unrealistic and often-times unhealthy demands of the contemporary masculine role.

This simple idea that men and women should be treated equally by society's institutions, has farreaching implications for societies around the globe. The United States has long been an arena engaged in the struggle for gender equity and can be contrasted with other cultures where the struggles are more entrenched and often more deadly. Looking at this issue from a cross-cultural and a historical perspective can demonstrate how peacemaking is concerned with ideas that have a broader context than simply the American criminal justice system. Gender roles are embedded into the very social fabric of cultures. It is impossible to examine how women are treated in the Middle East without an understanding of the Islamic religion. It is futile to look at the way women are treated in China without an appreciation for the ancient and recent history of that country. It is problematic to consider the role of women in the United States without grasping the impact capitalism has on efforts of social change. In short, feminism cannot be linked to the peacemaking perspective without a deep appreciation of how cultural, economic, and social systems have shaped and constrained the relationships between women and men. Therefore, our comments here need to be qualified as only suggestive of the impact of gender roles. A full understanding of feminism takes more space than available for our present purposes of simply identifying the issues.

In order to understand feminism, we must expand our way of thinking to realize that schools of thought can sometimes require fundamental life-changing challenges. For example, in defining feminism M. Kay Harris argues:

> Feminism offers and is a set of values, beliefs, and experiences—
> a consciousness, a way of looking at the world. Feminism should
> be seen not merely as a prescription for granting rights to women,
> but as a far broader vision. There are a number of varying strands
> within feminist thought, but there are some core values that tran-
> scend the differences. Among the key tenets of feminism are three
> simple beliefs—that all people have value as human beings, that
> harmony and felicity are more important than power and posses-
> sion, and that the personal is the political . . .[1]

Feminism, therefore, is not simply a political theme, but rather, a new way of looking at the relations between women and men as those relations exist in the context of social, economic, and political systems. The exact way those relations are envisioned is linked to the type of feminism that is adopted. The differences between types of feminism are significant, but, as Harris points out, there are key tenets that cut across all the variations.

Feminism can be envisioned in many ways. One method to differentiate between the variations is to look at the 12 types of feminism identified by Lorber.[2] Each type presents questions, issues, and concerns that guide its underlying feminist philosophy. For example, developmental feminism is concerned with the problems of women in developing countries, which are in many ways different than those in the United States. Lorber suggests:

For *developmental feminism,* the theoretical emphasis on universal human rights is reflected in developing countries in political pressure for the education of girls, maternity and child health care, and economic resources for women who contribute heavily to the support of their families. However, when feminist gender politics calls for wives and husbands to be equal, and for women to have sexual autonomy, developmental feminism frequently has to confront traditional cultural values and practices that give men power over their daughters and wives. The women's own solution to this dilemma is community organizing around their family roles.[3]

Clearly, when it comes to feminism, one size does not fit all. The state of development of the country, the religious context of the culture, the social status of the family, and the differences in the level of education between husband and wife and father and daughter all mediate the types of opportunities and roles that are afforded women. Equally important are the conscious decisions women make in deciding to become involved in conventional society. These types of feminism argue that conformity is too high a price to be paid for fundamental human rights. There should be tolerance for diversity in societies that are just, and that put the welfare of all citizens, particularly the "least of those," above the religious or moral systems of those who happen to be in power.

In this light, feminism can be seen as a natural tradition from which criminology peacemaking is derived. The concern for the individual caught up in the power of the dominant society speaks to both the fight against paternalism and such policies as the war on crime. When the state sanctions policies that deny equality to individuals, it is only reasonable for citizens to complain. In that complaint, however, new ways of relationships are suggested by both the many forms of feminism and peacemaking criminology. For instance, they converge on issues such as rape, domestic violence, gender discrimination in employment in the criminal justice system, and treatment of sex offenders. Additionally, problems such as the international trafficking in women and girls have been addressed by both feminists and peacemaking criminologists. The concern for both nonviolence and social justice are cornerstones of feminism and peacemaking criminology. Using domination to eliminate domination is an oxymoron. It's like the old 1960s saying about "fighting for peace." Feminism argues for new ways of knowing based on cooperation instead of conflict. The same can be said for peacemaking criminology.

There are a number of women whose work in peacemaking criminology flows from their commitment to feminist values and practices. M. Kay Harris is a university professor who has had extensive experience working in agencies that form crime control policies. She writes:

> A feminist orientation leads to greater awareness of the role and responsibility of society, not just the individual, in the development of conflict. This suggests that individuals, groups, and societies need to accept greater responsibility for preventing and reducing those conditions, values, and structures that produce violence and strife. Removing the idea of power from its central position is key here, and this requires continually challenging actions, practices, and assumptions that glorify power, control, and domination, as well as developing more felicitous alternatives.[4]

Another feminist who can be considered a peacemaking criminologist is M. Joan McDermott. McDermott argues that there is a link between one's personal life and social awareness and responsibility. To her, peacemaking at the personal level should be extended to the institutional and global levels. The connectedness of both peacemaking criminology and feminism are seen in her work:

> Ethical concerns and priorities of criminology as peacemaking are similar to those of feminist ethics, and these include. . . : We are all tied to other human beings and also the environment. To achieve peace and justice, we need loving and compassionate individuals. We also need equality. From love and compassion flow understanding, service, and justice. The nonviolent ethic assumes that human action is motivated by emotion as well as reason, and that knowledge is both rational and emotional.[5]

Peacemaking criminology shares many of its values, perspectives, and prac-titioners with the feminist perspective. Many would hesitate to make a dis-tinction between them and would object to being identified as one and not the other. They are not mutually exclusive points of view. In many ways, peacemaking criminology can be expressed as feminism that is applied to the problem of crime and the criminal justice system. But while they share many characteristics, peacemaking and feminism are not the same con-cept. Peacemaking criminology includes ideas from feminism, but does not mimic it. In fact, feminism draws much of its evolution from secular and humanist traditions. Peacemaking criminology also includes ideas from other intellectual traditions. As we have demonstrated in Chapter 2, peace-making criminology, in addition to feminism, looks to religious and human-ist intellectual traditions for inspiration and guidance. There is a third intel-lectual tradition identified by Pepinsky and Quinney that gives life to peacemaking criminology: the critical intellectual tradition.[6]

Critical Traditions

The critical intellectual tradition that informs peacemaking criminolo-gy covers a wide range of issues, theories, and perspectives. In the intro-ductory essay of his book of readings titled, *Social Justice, Criminal Justice*, Bruce Arrigo does an excellent job not only of listing, but of showing the rela-tionships between, the various strains of critical theory in law, crime, and deviance.[7] While recognizing that there are countless variations of critical criminology, Arrigo's book details 12 important and distinct types: Marxism, social feminism, peacemaking, prophetic criticism, anarchism, postmodern feminism, semiotics, constitutive criminology, critical race theory, chaos, cat-astrophe/topology, and queer theory.

Each of these critical perspectives examines ways in which individuals are oppressed by society and how this oppression is related to the problems of crime. Critical criminology is very much a macro-level analysis of soci-ety's contribution to the formulation of the crime problem and just as impor-tantly, of the implications of how society responds to crime. As the crimi-nal justice system is a tool of the powerful to maintain their interests, crime control can be looked at as an instrument of repression. The critical analy-sis of how the state uses the criminal justice system to selectively protect the interests of some individuals while selectively oppressing others, is at the heart of the critical intellectual tradition in criminology.

Arrigo situates the emergence of critical criminology in the works of Karl Marx. Marxism as a social philosophy is the intellectual father of all 11 vari-ations of critical criminology in his book. While peacemaking criminology is not as indebted to Marxism as other critical traditions, it does owe some of its orientation to this way of analyzing crime and conflict. Before we detail just how peacemaking criminology is related to Marxism, it is useful to understand just how fundamental Marxism is to the understanding of how crime and social control are problems located at the level of society and institutions rather than only at the level of the individual. For example, David Greenburg writes:

> To study crime in relation to the way societies organize their economic and political institutions is to ask different sorts of questions about crime than have typically been asked in non-Marxist criminology. Marxists do not deny that social-psychological processes and face-to-face interactions may have some importance for understanding crime and criminal justice, but they try to see these as shaped by larger social structures. And in characterizing these structures, they give particular attention to the organization of economic activity, without neglecting the political and ideological dimensions of society. Thus the Marxist perspective directs criminological theory "outward" rather than "inward."[8]

Critical criminology as it follows its Marxist heritage will look at how the economic arrangements and social organizations of a society will contribute to its crime problems. Marx was interested in the contradictions of capitalism and how the workers were exploited by those who owned the means of production. While many contemporary criminologists take capitalism as an unexamined background assumption, the critical criminologist will examine the economic system as a structural feature that mediates how the individual relates to society. Peacemaking criminology does not emphasize the economic dimension as much as some of the other variations of critical criminology, but views it as a genuine concern. Peacemaking criminologists are interested in the causes of suffering and in ways of relieving the pain of both victims and offenders, and the economic system is an important variable that can shed light on the constraints and possibilities of social and individual change.

For peacemaking criminology, however, the economic system is just one factor in the struggle for justice. Arrigo points out the distinction between *instrumental* and *structural* Marxism. Instrumental Marxists do see the economy as the primary factor in the development of crime and society's response to crime. Critical criminology perspectives such as left realists, social feminists, and postmodern criminologists are influenced by the emphasis on the economy of instrumental Marxism. On the other hand, structural Marxists see other forces such as politics, education, personal beliefs, and morality to be underlying structures that influence how a society develops definitions about crime, deviance, and law. Here, according to Arrigo, peacemaking criminology shares its heritage with other critical perspectives such as critical race theory and anarchist criminology.

Peacemaking criminology is sometimes faulted for drawing some of its heritage from Marxism that is associated with revolution.[9] The question is asked, how can peacemaking criminology arise out of a perspective that advocates violence as a way of seeking justice? This confusion arises from a misunderstanding about how intellectual traditions influence peacemaking. The idea of violence as a justified action is not supported by peacemaking criminology. For example, Gandhi and Martin Luther King, Jr., were both revolutionaries of a sort, but they stubbornly met violence with nonviolence. Just because some ideas are derived from Marxism doesn't mean that all of Marxism applies to peacemaking criminology. The Marxist tradition is just one area from which peacemaking criminology draws inspiration, and there are other intellectual traditions such as the religious and feminist that offer different proscriptions on the efficacy of violent behavior. One should not confuse Marxism with peacemaking criminology simply because they sometimes travel on the same road.

For some students, the term Marxism has extremely negative connotations. It is associated with communism, which we have been taught is evil. In our capitalistic state we are socialized to believe that other economic systems are not only inferior, but that the people who choose those systems are somehow bad people. Without getting into an extended debate about the relative merits of capitalism, socialism, and communism, we would like to suggest that a critical analysis of the problems of crime and the criminal justice system would be incomplete without recognizing that the economic organization of a society is a legitimate and important area to study. To exclude capitalism from the study of crime would be like playing football and saying that no one may tackle the quarterback. Marxist thought looks at the contradictions in the capitalist system that contribute to crime. Critical criminology perspectives, including peacemaking criminology, look at capitalism, as well as a host of other features of society, in their attempts to understand crime and formulate criminal justice policy. An intellectually honest football player must tackle anyone who has the ball, even if it is sometimes his own quarterback.

A Peacemaking Criminology Perspective

Just as we have seen that there are many ways that Marxist thought can be used to examine the issues of crime and the criminal justice system, so too, are there many ways that peacemaking criminology can be constructed. What we present here is just one way that makes sense to us. As peacemaking is relatively new to the study of crime, it is still evolving. We do not claim that what we present here will be definitive. Our conception of peacemaking criminology is only suggestive of one way of looking at the important issues. We present here the structure of peacemaking criminology used by Fuller in his book, *Criminal Justice: A Peacemaking Perspective*[10] In a later chapter we will apply this perspective to the field of corrections.

Figure 3.1
Peacemaking Pyramid Paradigm

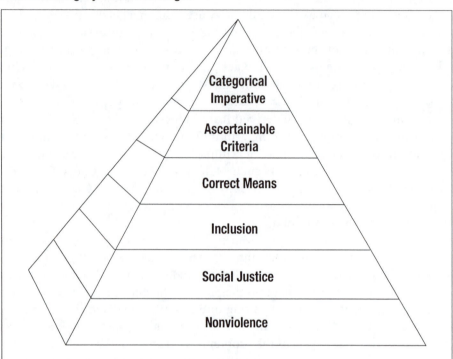

Fuller envisioned peacemaking criminology as a pyramid of ideas. He calls this model the Peacemaking Pyramid Paradigm. At the base of the pyramid is the foundation of nonviolence. Following the ideas of Christ, Tolstoy, Gandhi, and Martin Luther King, Jr., and other saints and sages, any proposal that advocates or tolerates violence as a response to infractions of the law cannot be considered a peacemaking perspective. State violence such as excessive use of police force, capital punishment, corporal punishment, or any such idea that citizens can be punished into conformity is outside the bounds of peacemaking criminology. A state that models the violence it is trying to prevent is engaged in a vicious, self-perpetuating cycle of pain and suffering for all concerned. Violence begets violence and as a social and criminal justice policy, violence is doomed to failure and carries with it far-reaching consequences.

After nonviolence, the next criteria necessary for a peacemaking perspective, is social justice. Even when cases are resolved in a nonviolent manner, if the underlying social justice that gave rise to the problem remains, the solution can't be considered to be in keeping with the peacemaking perspective. Peacemaking should not be confused with peacekeeping. Peacemaking is a more comprehensive concept that attempts to resolve the underlying issues that gave rise to the conflict. For example, in the case of a juvenile who continually bullies his classmates, it would not be enough to simply move the young man to another classroom. Peacemaking would entail repairing the relationship between the bully and his victims. The bully must learn to understand how his behavior causes suffering, and the victims must have their concerns addressed and not act out bullying behaviors on other younger and weaker victims. Peacemaking strives to solve the problem through social justice, not simply sweep it under the rug. This idea is currently being expanded as demonstrated in the restorative and community justice movement.

A third principle of the peacemaking perspective is inclusion. All who are affected by a criminal justice system decision should be included in its making. This means not just the state, but the victim(s), the offender, the community, and even some more tangentially affected parties, such as the offender's family or school officials. All who are harmed by the violation or are significant agents for positive change in the offender's life should be eligible for inclusion in the resolution of the case. This means the offender should have some input into the sentence. In order for the sentence to be more than simple punishment, and for it to help transform and rehabilitate, the offender needs to have his or her voice heard. There is an added benefit of this concept of inclusion and that is the dividends accrued from community participation in the process. Fuller puts it this way:[11]

> From a peacemaking perspective, this involvement of the offender and the victims in the process can do much toward revitalizing the trust citizens have in their ability to govern themselves. When the victim and the offender are pawns in the games played by the courtroom work group they become disenfranchised. When mandatory sentences are decided by the legislature, the criminal justice system practitioners become also become distanced and alienated from the process. In our rush to remove discretion from the criminal court system, we have also removed the attachments that bond individuals to the process and the outcomes. From a peacemaking perspective, what is needed is a way to bring people back into the system.

The next step on the pyramid is the concept of correct means. This idea is found in many religious traditions and argues that the end, however desirable, does not justify immoral means. Applied to the criminal justice system, this idea of correct means would include the principle that the offenders be given their constitutional and human rights. Law enforcement officers should adhere to the procedural law that dictates how they detect crime and arrest offenders. Correct means entails the idea that the determination of outcomes is as important as the outcomes themselves. The process should be a model of the desired outcome. Gandhi was a champion of the notion of "correct means" and supported the idea that we must "become" the change that we want to see in our community and our world. This is no less true for the criminal justice system. Correct means requires the criminal justice system to be the paragon of fairness and virtue. This is a difficult concept for some criminal justice practitioners to accept. Because offenders often lie in addition to committing their other crimes, it is believed by some that trickery and subterfuge are acceptable means to use in the criminal justice system. The procedural law that dictates how law enforcement officers do their jobs is crafted to prevent abuse of the means of enforcement. The law is sometimes viewed as "getting in the way" or "tying the hands of the police." The procedural law protects all citizens from overzealous police officers. While dealing fairly and justly with criminals is a difficult and challenging task, the vast majority of police officers are conscientious professionals. There are, however, some who are not professional in the way they administer justice, but may be so negligent of the procedural law that they violate the legal, and sometimes human, rights of citizens. The arrest of Rodney King in Los Angeles is a good example of incorrect means.

The fifth step in the Peacemaking Pyramid Paradigm is ascertainable criteria. This idea is taken from a useful book on negotiating conflict titled *Getting to Yes*.[12] One of the principles of the book is that of using objective criteria. This means that if there is a dispute about the price of a house, an independent appraisal can be conducted to fix a price upon which everyone can agree. In the Peacemaking Pyramid Paradigm, ascertainable criteria expands on this idea by ensuring the means of justice are not only objective, but are actually understood by all concerned. The legal jargon of the criminal justice system is not understood by many. Individuals are processed through the system with little understanding of how or when they agreed to give up legal rights. It is useful to the criminal justice system as well as other professions, to employ complicated criteria and unintelligible parlance. Those who do not understand cannot object to incorrect means. If all offenders were lawyers, the use of highly technical and legal language would not be a problem. In the criminal justice system, however, most of the offenders do not understand what is happening, and it is desirable to educate them to the process so they can feel they have been treated fairly.

Finally, the Peacemaking Pyramid Paradigm advocates the Kantian concept of the categorical imperative. Simply put, the categorical imperative says that every action should be considered as if it would become a universal law. In other words, I cannot be willing to have something done to you that I would not be willing to have done to myself. This would ensure a certain consistency to how our laws are enforced and give individuals a clear idea of where the boundaries of appropriate behavior are drawn and enforced. Additionally, the categorical imperative can be applied to the peacemaking perspective according to the following:

> From a peacemaking perspective, this means that solutions to
> particular criminal justice problems should entail underlying
> moral reasoning so that the solution would be applicable in other

times and places. Kant's categorical imperative attempts to establish principles that transcend the particular circumstances of individual cases and can serve as guides to moral behavior.[13]

As can be seen, the Peacemaking Pyramid Paradigm attempts to include a number of peacemaking principles and organize them in a way that demonstrates a comprehensive process of envisioning peace in the criminal justice system. There are certainly other ways of conceptualizing a peacemaking philosophy that can be applied to the criminal justice system, but we find the Peacemaking Pyramid Paradigm sufficient for our needs to explore how peacemaking can be applied to corrections. In fact, corrections is one of the areas of the justice system that has tremendous potential for adopting the peacemaking perspective.

Levels of Peacemaking

One of the strengths of the peacemaking perspective lies in its applicability and integration to many levels of analysis. The peacemaking perspective can be envisioned at the intrapersonal, interpersonal, institutional/societal, and the international/global levels. While our focus on corrections is on the first three of these levels, there is certainly an opportunity to link peacemaking to the international/global level as we consider how we should proactively respond to correct problems with other countries and how other countries choose to deal with offenders. Briefly, the levels of analysis of the peacemaking perspective are important because of the way they form a seamless web of thought and action for the problems of crime, social order, and justice.

The intrapersonal dimension is concerned with how individuals think about themselves. Their sense of who they are is a powerful contributor to their behavior. Thoreau said, "most men lead lives of quiet desperation." For some offenders, their lives are not so quiet and are punctuated by acts of extreme violence. It is the opinion of one psychiatrist who has worked extensively with violent inmates that an underlying problem is their feelings of shame.

> I have yet to see a serious act of violence that was not provoked by the experience of feeling shamed and humiliated, disrespected and ridiculed, and that did not attempt to prevent or undo this "loss of face"—no matter how severe the punishment, even if it includes death. For we misunderstand these men at our own peril, if we do not realize that they mean it literally when they say they would rather kill or mutilate others, be killed or mutilated themselves, than live without pride, dignity, and self-respect. They literally prefer death to dishonor.[14]

This intrapersonal dimension is a key and a possible starting point to the understanding of how we might approach the rehabilitation of offenders. While some critics of the peacemaking perspective might contend that we should not care if offenders see potential value or worth in themselves or not, but that we should only worry about their behavior, the peacemaking perspective argues that how individuals feel about themselves in relation to others is a primary determinant of their behavior.[15]

The interpersonal dimension deals with how we relate to each other in our daily lives. The peacemaking perspective has relevance here as a guide for harmony, togetherness, and intimacy. Whether it is a spouse, child, co-worker, fellow inmate, or total stranger, the peacemaking perspective suggests that your interactions be based on trust, fairness, kindness, and compassion. For too many of us, the pressures of competition in a perceived zero-sum game prevent us from interacting in a positive and co-operational way with others.

The institutional/societal level of the peacemaking perspective includes the criminal justice system and, of course, corrections. It also includes many other arenas of potential conflict such as the family, school, and workplace. The way we structure our social institutions can have profound effects on how people behave. When we allow racism or sexual (or other kinds of) harassment to be tolerated in our schools and businesses, we invite reactions that may be violent. When we do not allow equal opportunity and social justice, we invite fraud and deceit. In the corrections system, we invite violence and conflict for offenders and correctional staff alike, when we allow inmates to be brutalized by correctional officers and each other. We model killing for society when we employ capital punishment. By changing the way we operate our institutions, we can began to have a more positive impact on how we relate to each other. It is a reciprocal process.

At the international/global level the peacemaking perspective has a well-recognized tradition. The prevention and resolution of armed international conflicts is a major concern for organizations like the United Nations. While some might claim there are still plenty of wars in the world, it seems clear that there could be even more but for the efforts of organizations and individuals who actively work to resolve conflicts. The Camp David Accord is an example of peacemaking that has maintained the peace between Israel and Egypt for many years. The international/global level of the peacemaking perspective can also be applied to the environment (as can the other levels). Human beings must learn to live in harmony with the environment for their long-term survival. There are concerns by many that the environment is being destroyed in many parts of the world with the results being unsafe air, water, and scarcity of food. Additionally, there are longer-term, complex problems such as global warming and the destruction of important resources such as the Amazon rain forest that have more than just a local or regional impact. It was Buckminster Fuller who coined the term spaceship earth to illustrate how interdependent we all have become.

Crime and Peace

It has been our intention in this chapter to demonstrate the applicability of the peacemaking perspective to the criminal justice system. We have done this by outlining two intellectual traditions from which the peacemaking perspective draws inspiration. The feminist and critical traditions challenge the power structures of contemporary society. Crime and criminal justice are very much about how power is distributed and used in this society, as we will demonstrate in a following chapter.

A peacemaking perspective that presents a comprehensive paradigm of how peace principles can be applied at many levels of analysis has also been outlined. This perspective, while just one way to envision how peacemaking can be focused on the criminal justice system, has the advantage of illustrating how interconnected the personal and political realms of life actually are.

Finally, we would suggest that peacemaking criminology is increasingly becoming a major perspective in our thinking about crime. We will demonstrate how through processes such as alternative dispute resolution and restorative justice, that peacemaking criminology is more than just an academic curiosity. In the real world of crime, criminals, and society's response to issues of social control, the peacemaking perspective is a viable and powerful choice.

Questions

1. Identify the three major traditions from which peacemaking criminology evolved. Discuss how these traditions share many of the same concepts. What aspects of each tradition does peacemaking criminology not endorse?

2. Discuss the Peacemaking Pyramid Paradigm. How does this figure help in envisioning the peacemaking perspective? Are there aspects of peacemaking that this paradigm ignores? If you were assigned to visually demonstrate the peacemaking perspective, what would your figure look like?

3. The chapter contends that the peacemaking perspective can be applied to four levels of understanding: intrapersonal, interpersonal, institutional, and societal. Which of these levels do you feel is important? Why?

4. What commonalities can you see between the feminist and critical traditions and the humanist and religious traditions of peacemaking criminology? Is there a seamless web running through all these traditions or are there dislocations and contradictions?

5. Is peacemaking criminology a liberal or conservative way to address the problems of the criminal justice system?

Notes

1   Harris, M. Kay "Moving into the New Millennium: Toward a Feminist Vision of Justice." In Harold Pepinsky and Richard Quinney (eds.) (1991). *Criminology as Peacemaking.* Bloomington, IN: Indiana University Press, pp. 83-97.

2   Lorber, Judith (1998). *Gender Inequality: Feminist Theories and Politics* Los Angeles: Roxbury Publishing Company. Lorber identifies 12 types of feminism: liberal, Marxist and socialist, developmental, radical, lesbian, psychoanalytic, standpoint, multiracial, men's, social construction, and postmodern and queer theory.

3   Lorber, p. 16.

4   Harris, p. 93.

5   McDermott, M. Joan. "From a Peacemaking Perspective, Is Personal Change More Important Than Social Change? No." In John R. Fuller and Eric W. Hickey (eds.) (1999). *Controversial Issues in Criminology.* Boston, MA: Allyn and Bacon, pp. 119-126.

6   Pepinsky, Harold and Richard Quinney (eds.) (1991). *Criminology as Peacemaking.* Bloominton, IN: Indiana University Press.

7   Arrigo, Bruce A. (1999). *Social Justice, Criminal Justice: The Maturation of Critical Theory in Law, Crime, and Deviance.* Belmont, CA: West/Wadsworth.

8   Greenburg, David F. (1981). *Crime and Capitalism: Readings in Marxist Criminology.* Palo Alto, CA: Mayfield Publishing, p. 18.

9   Akers, Ronald L. (1997). *Criminological Theories: Introduction and Evaluation*, Second Edition. Los Angeles, CA: Roxbury Publishing Company.

10 Fuller, John R. (1998). *Criminal Justice: A Peacemaking Perspective*. Boston, MA: Allyn and Bacon.

11 Fuller, p. 121.

12 Fisher, Roger, William Ury and Bruce Patton (1995). *Getting to Yes*, Second Edition. New York, NY: Penguin Books.

13 Fuller, p. 57.

14 Gilligan, James (1996). *Violence: Reflections on a National Epidemic* New York, NY: Vintage Books.

15 These critics include, Gendreau, Paul (1996). "Offender Rehabilitation: What We Know and What Needs to Be Done." *Criminal Justice and Behavior,* 23:144-161. Ross, R. and Gendreau, P. (1980). *Effective Correctional Treatment*. Toronto, CN: Butterworth.

Part II
Doing Peacemaking

*"We meet ourselves time and again in a thousand disguises
on the path of life."*
– Carl Jung

Freedom is what you do with what's been done to you.
– Jean-Paul Sartre

*. . . If I love all that I can this day, if I laugh all that I can this day,
if I give all the happiness I can this day, if I do the least amount of bad that
I can this day, then when this day comes back to me, I won't want
to change it even if I could.*
– Sam Johnson, Death Row inmate

Chapter 4
Personal Transformation

Introduction

From the beginning, the most important work has been about helping people to make "The Big Change"—deep, genuine, personal, and spiritual transformation.

A friend of one of the authors was posed an interesting question: Are we physical beings having a spiritual experience or spiritual beings having a physical experience? In the context of our "timeless" journey and our quest for peace, it is the latter. The main difference between a spiritual path and a typical contemporary strategy for personal happiness is that one is about the self, and the other is about moving beyond that very self. The bigger journey is not about being comfortable or nice or safe. It is not primarily about living in a supportive environment. We may need some special support for a while, but when genuine transformation happens, we are able to go anywhere, be among any kind of people, and not be distracted from our sense of peace and goodwill.

While such transformation can be pursued through theistic, nontheistic, or atheistic perspectives, including searching for a sense of meaning and moral purpose through relationships or a sense of the transcendent, we have chosen to focus on a spiritual context consistent with the wisdom traditions we discussed in Chapter 2.[1]

The great Indian saint Ramakrishna likened our journey to the life of an oak tree: In the beginning, it may need a lot of care and tenderness, it may even need a little fence around it to keep it from being trampled on, but when it grows into its full stature, with its roots deep into the earth, the tree can provide shade for countless travelers and it needs nothing in return. That's the potential we all share.

A Voice in the Wilderness

In our current age, we are constantly bombarded by seductive messages to avoid pain, avoid struggle, take a pill to get rid of this, get divorced to get rid of that, and put our own happiness above all other concerns. We have come to believe that we are *entitled* to everything and *responsible* for nothing. If life becomes too difficult or too painful, we are inclined to look for the easiest way to bail out.

The timeless spiritual message is always a voice crying in the wilderness: *Life is about something more wonderful than you can imagine. Don't be afraid. This whole world is not what it appears to be. Wake up to your true nature. Wake up and rejoice.*

When we are in a miserable prison—either self-made, or one of bars and steel—or when we are steeped in our addictions or compulsions that we continue to engage in even though they may be destroying our lives, those timeless spiritual messages may seem so remote from our daily reality that they strike us as being totally irrelevant. However, that is precisely the time it may be most important to remember: *Keep trying. Do the practices. Study hard. Pray for help. Be willing to change. Make an effort. Persevere.*

A prison friend once told one of the authors that sometimes we may be hanging on by a thread, but that thread may be enough to keep us from giving up. Life is always going to be loss and gain, pleasure and pain, pride and shame. Everyone has tough times. Life is pretty hard. Everyone struggles.

The great tragedy of our times is that the vast majority of people, especially our youth, seem to feel they are struggling for nothing. Imagine how hopeless and weary they become. The seeker struggles too, struggles constantly, but with faith that life is intelligent, not chaotic; that life can be merciful, not cruel.[2]

Dying to Self

If only we could have what we want and not have to *change* so much for it! "God, I'm a decent person at heart. Oh, sure, I have faults, but I don't mean anyone any harm. Why can't you just help my life to work better? Why does everything have to be so *hard*?" Why must life require so much constant work? Why must change require so much *change*? Or as Father Kelty put our personal and spiritual journey in context: ". . . This whole dialogue runs deep in us and all things. One could say, with complete honesty, that life is really no more than a series of heart-breaking good-byes, so full is it of having and letting go, of embracing and parting."

As strange as it may seem, we take comfort from all of this. If our lives seem to be a ceaseless procession of hurdles requiring us to jump higher and higher, we do not have to feel so alone. Sages and saints throughout the ages have assured us there is a great purpose to all of this; it's *not* just "Life's a bitch and then you die." Once we surrender to what life is really about, which is a spiritual and personally transforming journey, then we find there is plenty of advice, instruction, and comfort amid the difficulties. When we take the advice of the great religious and wisdom traditions, we discover that the majority of our obstacles and pain are caused by us in the first place.

It's easy to call oneself a Christian or a Jew, a Buddhist or Muslim or Hindu, or Taoist, but it's another thing entirely to really live according to the teachings of any genuine religion, wisdom, or philosophical tradition. Christ said that many will come in His name, but we must look for the ones actually doing His Father's work. When the American sage Joseph Campbell was asked whom he considered to be the greatest living Christian, he replied, "His Holiness the Dalai Lama." The Dalai Lama is the leader of Tibetan Buddhism; he's not considered to be a Christian at all. Campbell was using Jesus's own instructions about who is and who isn't a Christian; the Dalai Lama's life is entirely dedicated to compassion, mercy, love, justice, charity, humility, forgiveness—all the qualities that Jesus described as His Father's work.

Many people go to church on Sunday or special religious days and then pass by a beggar on their way home without stopping to help in any way. They choose a place of worship which will comfort them in a self-centered lifestyle rather than challenge them to be true to their tradition. Being a true Christian is a terrifying prospect. Being a true Buddhist, Jew, or anything else is a terrifying prospect. All the religions stress that we must die as self-centered persons in order to discover new life as selfless, loving, generous, fearless souls.

Die to my own plans and dreams? Die to my countless preferences and aversions? Die to my pride and greed? Yes, yes, and yes, Die.

Father Murray Rogers, the beloved elder on the board of directors for the Human Kindness Foundation, had a powerful experience along these lines many years ago. Father Murray is a Christian who has been involved in the interfaith dialogue for more than 50 years. As part of his interfaith experience, he went to Japan to spend time in a Zen Buddhist temple for a few months. The Temple was a serenely beautiful place, extremely neat and orderly, extremely quiet, like most Zen temples.

The abbot, a small, courteous man of few words, showed Murray around for a half-hour or more, whispering "This is where you will eat," "This is where you will be meditating," "This is your room" and so forth. In his room, just before turning to leave, the abbot leaned forward toward Murray and whispered, "There is just one more thing." And then he thrust his face directly into Murray's with a wild look and screamed at the top of his lungs, *"YOU MUST DIE!!!!!"*

The abbot turned and left, with young Murray trembling like a leaf, thinking, "Oh, no, I've gotten myself into some bizarre cult, this man is crazy, what do I do now?" and so forth. But after a while, as the adrenaline settled and his mind regained a little composure, Murray began to think, "Well, isn't that actually what Jesus said as well? 'You must die to self and be born again of

Spirit?' Perhaps I have just never taken it seriously before. Perhaps this Zen Master is not so crazy after all. Perhaps Zen and Christianity are not so different. Every Christian prayer I have ever uttered is essentially my willingness to die and be reborn in Christ."

Father Murray did complete his stay in the Zen Temple. Today he is an 81-year-old joyful and humble Christian elder who has recognized that this message of dying into Christ is found in one form or another in all the great religions and wisdom traditions.

No sage or prophet has suggested that this "dying into life" is fun. That is why being a good Christian or anything else is a truly challenging idea. We are called upon to actually give our lives away in duty, service, devotion; to worship God through kindness to His creation. Jesus was not vague about this at all; He made it crystal-clear: "Whatever you have done for the least of my brethren, you have done for me."

In the free world, "the least of my brethren" include the growing numbers of homeless people, the hookers and ex-cons, the crippled and disfigured. In prison, the "least of my brethren" would apply to sex-offenders, homosexuals, snitches. Anywhere we ever find ourselves, there will be a population we can conveniently exclude from our glance, from our friendship, from our respect; a population we can look down upon and feel superior to.

If Jesus appeared in a prison today, He would offer His friendship to the very lowest inmates on the totem pole, and many who claim to be Christians would criticize and scorn Him for it. According to the teachings of Jesus, "*everyone* is invited to My Father's table."

That, of course, does not mean everyone accepts the invitation, but that is not our business. It is our business to be respectful to all, open to all, no matter what they look like or what they may have done in the past. "Judge not, lest ye be judged." And most of us have plenty to be judged for! When one of the authors was teaching a class on prisons, a small vocal group of students when asked why they were so strongly in favor of severely punishing inmates, responded that they wanted the inmates to "get what they deserved." The teacher paused briefly, then quietly requested that everyone in the class who wanted to "get what they deserved" to please raise their hands. Not a single hand was raised. Whatever the context, we are inclined to want retribution when we are the victim, and forgiveness when we are the offender. In the same class, the teacher proposed a scenario and asked the class to make a difficult choice: (1) they could be the offender who seriously injured an innocent victim or (2) they could be the victim, who would recover, but not before enduring severe, extended pain. In response to the assignment, most students indicated that while they did not want to injure anyone, if it came down to it, they would hurt someone else rather than allow themselves to be injured. Then a shy coed raised her hand and stated that even though she would be severely injured, she would choose to be the victim. When the teacher asked why, she replied, "because only the victim has the power to forgive."

It is very easy to fall into hatred, superiority, and racism, especially in a place like prison, where we hardly have any power over who does what to whom. But easy or not, it is important that we resist the impulse. Keeping a daily discipline of practices and readings can help a great deal by giving us a bigger view than what we see on the prison yard or in the corporate office.

True tolerance and respect are not easy in today's world. For example, the Christmas Story is not an easy story: The perfect child, the Lamb of God, the Prince of Peace, is born in a barn among cattle, then has to be hidden in foreign lands for many years, then comes out to get scorned and crucified. What was easy or fair about that? And He was innocent!

You and I have done many wrong things, many selfish things which have hurt others, and yet our life is still easier than the life of Jesus or countless other sages. He and other saints showed us that Love is superior to power, yet we constantly struggle for power in our lives rather than open ourselves into that Love. He showed us the way which leads to life and the way which leads to death, and we continue to choose death in its many forms, over life.

The world is very much in need right now for ordinary men and women like ourselves to take the great teachings seriously. Anger, selfishness, and political and religious divisiveness are destroying our planet. It's time to *be* the teachings instead of discussing and debating them. "No greater love has a person than to lay down his or her life for someone else." And what happens when we do? That's the Great Irony: We discover all the freedom, peace, and hope we had been unsuccessfully trying to find through selfish living.[3]

When Everything Goes Wrong: The Case of William

Today approximately 48,000 people each month are being released from American prisons. A friend of one of the authors got out of prison on the last day of 1997. He was 37 years old and had been in prison since he was 19. Because he was on a 90-year sentence, he had spent his whole prison time in one old maximum-security facility in mid-Florida that has a very tough reputation.

In all those years, William (not his real name) was never encouraged to get a G.E.D. or any other education or skills training. There were few programs offered at his prison. Because all the inmates there had such long sentences, the state wasn't inclined to invest resources for education and related programs.

When the state did release him, they let him out the gate with a short-sleeved shirt and $50. This scenario is repeated every day all over the United States. It's an embarrassment and a mockery of the idea that the state is giving persons like William a "second chance." How much of a chance does he have with $50 and no skills or education?

But William had practiced meditation for many years while he was inside, and after improving his reading skills, he studied a number of spiritual books. He developed a prayer life. He became a quiet, kind person. So he had no intention, when he was released, of giving all that up and turning back to crime. He had made the Big Change. Crime was no longer an option he desired.

William was placed in contact with some caring people doing non-profit work in the community, and he found a place to live and work with them for awhile. He wasn't making much money, but he got room and board and began learning how to cook, bake bread, do some light carpentry, and occasionally speak to community groups about his own "before and after" story, which was very well received.

Because he had done so much spiritual practice in prison, William assumed he would have no difficulty adjusting to life outside of prison. Everyone else said, "After spending your whole adult life in a tough prison, you'll probably hit some hard challenges out here." But William would always smile and say he was just glad to be out, and nothing would be rough about life out here at all.

It was around February when the first wave of depression hit him. William had no idea what was going on. He slipped deeper and deeper into silence, shutting out the people around him just like he would have done in prison. But these people were his friends, not his jailers. They had been expecting him to hit some rough spots and they were ready to help him through them. But William did not yet know how to ask for or receive such help. He closed off and became grim. Everyone would try to talk with him, ask him questions, and he would respond in short, unfriendly grunts. And being tall and muscular and prison-hard, he could be pretty intimidating when he was feeling unfriendly.

He was experiencing a great deal of confusion and pride. William had no idea why he was depressed, and he was too proud to admit it. He had spent so many years fending for himself, trusting only himself, figuring everything out for himself, that he didn't know how to handle life in any other way. Several of his friends and co-workers became angry with him, taking his rejection personally. And of course, that made matters worse.

By March of 1998, William was actually saying, "Maybe I should just go back to prison." And he was also saying, "Every night when I go to sleep, I pray for God to let me die before I wake up. I have nothing to live for." Here's an intelligent, healthy, 38-year-old man with a whole lifetime of freedom opening up to him, and he just wanted to be back in prison or dead. Sad and amazing, but not surprising.

Things continued to get worse for William, and finally Bo had a few talks with him when it seemed that he was not going to be able to work through his despair by himself. His co-workers had already given him plenty of pep-talks, all to no avail. The only thing that came to Bo to say to him was this: "William, I want you to think very seriously about two simple questions. If you can truthfully answer 'yes' to both questions, then I know you're going to get through this. If your answers are 'no,' then I don't know what else to say to you. Here are the questions: (1) Does God know what you're going through? (2) Does God care?"

These two questions can be a self-test to see whether you are a person of "faith" or not. Pick out your biggest problem or obstacle in life. If you honestly believe that God knows and cares, then you are a person of faith. If you do not believe that God knows and cares, then you may feel that you have to face your despair from a cynic's vantage point; alone and unloved.

Bo knew that William was truly a spiritual person, and so for him, those two questions forced an undeniable "yes" on both counts. And once he admitted to himself that he does believe God knows and cares, then he no longer felt alone and no longer felt like he was just going crazy for no purpose at all. He realized that God must be pushing him to learn something and no matter how hard it was, he felt that God would help him through it.

In William's case, what he was being pushed to learn had to do with pride and with real friendship; being able to admit that he was scared and confused, being able to accept love from the people around him; not having to be Superman.

We may never understand completely why William broke down so deeply after several months' freedom. It could probably be explained in many different ways. It doesn't matter if one understands it as much as to face it with honesty, faith, and support from friends. That's what William finally did, and now he has been out for nearly two years. He has a good job and many friends.

Like all of us, he still occasionally has rough times. But he remembers the two questions. He remembers that his answers are "yes," and so he knows he's never alone or unloved. And that may be enough to get us through the rough times when nothing else seems to help.[4]

Faith

> *Go ahead, light your candles and burn your incense and ring your bells and call out to God, but watch out, because God will come, and He will put you on His Anvil and fire up His Forge and beat you and beat you until He turns brass into Pure Gold.*
> – paraphrased from Sant Keshavadas

The above quote may sound intimidating, but doesn't it also provide some comfort? Don't you and I often feel like we have had the hell beaten out of us by the unwanted situations or difficult people in our lives? We may feel bruised, defeated, exhausted, but then remember, "Is this what it feels like to be beaten and beaten until I am pure gold?" If we can take just the smallest bit of faith that way, maybe we can go on one more day. Faith is the key. But we so often misunderstand it and create a so-called faith which is more like a letter to Santa Claus for everything we want, and then when we don't get it, we "lose our faith."

Bo and Sita Lozoff, along with a few members of the Human Kindness staff, spent a day on death row in Raleigh, North Carolina. Bo gave a couple of talks and they were able to spend some time with the condemned men. One of them approached Bo to express his appreciation for the visit, and to share his glad tidings that Jesus had saved him. Now he knows that his next court appearance will go in his favor. He said Jesus will not allow him to be executed. He will be released from prison and reunited with his family. Jesus won't let him down. The fellow beamed and said he has "complete faith."

An elderly woman recently wrote one of the authors that she always had strong faith in God and was devoutly religious, but then she developed bladder cancer. Though she prayed, followed all the right regimens, and even traveled great distances to be blessed by holy sages, God did not fulfill her expectations. Her faith was shattered.

Does Jesus not love our condemned friend if the court upholds his execution? Is God betraying the prayers of the elderly woman if she dies of cancer?

Better Catch Up On Religious History

If we take even a brief look at the history of the great world religions, it becomes clear that faith and religion have more to do with our response to things going wrong than with our problems being magically set right.

> • **Faith is a profound acceptance of life's Ultimate Goodness no matter what happens.**

It's a willingness on our part to accept *any* immediate situation—execution, cancer, loss, betrayal—as part of God's power and Grace and Love for us, like the following story from the Sikh religion illustrates:

> One of the great Sikh warrior/gurus was captured by the invading Mughal army. The enemy emperor was very excited to have finally defeated one of the pillars of the Sikh faith. He summoned his soldiers to bring the prisoner to him.
>
> Bound in chains, the Sikh general was forced to his knees before the emperor. The emperor mocked him and said, "Let's see your great faith save you now!" The Sikh general calmly replied, "I can write down a magic formula which will shield me from all harm."
>
> The emperor was furious, and shouted, "Bring this lunatic a paper and pen!"
>
> The Sikh general wrote a few words, folded the paper and kept it in his hand. The emperor said, "Now, cut off his head!" A soldier raised his sharp sword, cut off the Sikh's head, and his body fell lifeless to the ground.
>
> The paper was taken from his hand and read aloud: "You can have my head, but not my Faith."

- **The Holy Ones of every religion came here to show us the way that a person of faith can respond, not to a world which supports or rewards our faith, but to a world which often despises, condemns, rejects, exiles, tortures, or even murders us for it.**

Jesus or Buddha didn't come to get us off of death row or heal our cancer or patch up our worldly problems. They came to inspire the courage in us to live as they did—to love others and dedicate our lives to the common good. Faith in such a way of life is a very radical choice, because it is opposite to nearly everything we have been taught. It can also be extremely unpopular. Jesus, Gandhi, and countless other sages have been killed for it.

But if we make that choice and stick to it, we will have the opportunity to touch something so incomprehensibly deep and loving that it no longer matters so much whether we spend the rest of our days behind bars or not.

Saint Stephen touched that Love, and it was so fulfilling that even as an angry mob stoned him to death shouting "Blasphemer!," all he could cry out was, "Father, please don't hold this against them."

Mahatma Gandhi touched that Love. As an assassin's bullet tore into his brain, his immediate response was, "Jai Ram!" ("Hail God!").

It Doesn't Always End Badly

When the Chinese invaded Tibet, they killed countless peaceful monks and destroyed most of the monasteries. One Chinese general was especially known for his barbaric cruelty of disemboweling monks with his sword while they screamed for mercy. At one remote monastery, word came that this particular general and his band of soldiers were on their way. All the monks fled to the hills except one elderly monk who sat calmly in the main hall.

When the general arrived and heard that one monk had not run in fear, he was enraged. He threw open the doors of the great hall, strode over to the small man and screamed, "DO YOU KNOW WHO I AM??! WHY, I COULD TAKE MY SWORD AT THIS VERY MOMENT, PLUNGE IT INTO YOUR BELLY AND REMOVE YOUR ORGANS WITHOUT BATTING AN EYE!!"

The elderly monk looked into the general's eyes and softly replied, "But do you know who *I* am? Why, I could allow you to take your sword at this very moment, plunge it into my belly and remove my organs, without batting an eye."

The general meekly lowered his eyes, bowed, backed away, and ordered his troops to leave the monastery at once.

So it's not that things always turn out badly. Indeed, every religion is full of such stories about the incredible power of pure faith. But it's a serious mistake to think that such outcomes are the point. They are not, and never have been, the point of faith. They are just *demonstrations* of the Power we're dealing with – not guarantees. The elderly monk in the story above was telling the truth: He really would have been just as calm and fearless if the general had indeed disemboweled him. His faith was not tied to a particular result. He knew the picture was much bigger than that.

> • **Miracle stories serve to remind us that if God wanted our problems to be miraculously solved, they would be. So if the court says, "Execute him," or the doctor says, "Sorry, ma'am, but you're not responding to treatment," or Pontius Pilate says, "Crucify Him," then we know that God had the power to change it and didn't. So we can walk calmly even through the valley of the shadow of death, knowing "Thou art with me." No bitterness, no doubts, no panic.**

The issue is not one of power. The power was available to save our death-row friend from execution, just as the way could have been easier for many sages and apostles. And of course God can cure cancer, and sometimes does. But not usually. Jesus didn't heal *all* the lame; He didn't give sight to *all* the blind; He didn't raise *all* the dead.

A friend of one of the authors was once suffering from kidney stones. One night when he was in unbearable pain, he cried out to Jesus, "Jesus, take this pain, please," and was startled to hear in response, "But I just *gave* it to you."

God creates beans, fire water, and a pot. God creates the principle that beans will taste better and be digested more easily when they're cooked. God creates the principle that water boils when heated with fire. Then it's up to us.

We have the power to abide or not abide by these principles of God's law, to use or not use them to make a good meal. We can choose to put the pot on our heads, eat raw beans, and pour the water onto the ground. We can do all sorts of things with the best of ingredients and the most wonderful natural laws.

> • **God's power designs and creates unlimited possibilities; our power is to bring the best of those possibilities to life in the world instead of the worst.**

Look around at the world. People say, "Why does God allow children to starve, why does God allow innocent people to be murdered, why does God allow so many wars? But God has merely created all possibilities, including the ingredients necessary for a miserable world or a wonderful world. We have the free will to use the ingredients in a way that will bring more peace or more suffering. That's our choice, yours and mine, all the time.

> *Past the seeker as he prayed, came the crippled and the beggar and the beaten. And seeing them, the holy one went down into deep prayer and cried, "Great God, how is it that a loving creator can see such things and yet do nothing about them?" And out of the long silence, God said, "I did do something. I made you."*
>
> – Sufi teaching story

We continue to choose anger over Love, fear over Love, national boundaries over Love, greed over Love, race over Love, self-protection over Love. God has given us Free Will so that we can make such choices. If we don't like the way the world is going, then we can begin to choose differently right now, today, right here, wherever we are. Waiting for everyone else to change first is a fool's game. Waiting for others to love us first, before we are willing to love them, is a fool's game. We can start where we are. One person at a time.

The Buddha said that the biggest mistake we can make is to want to be loved. How much we are loved by others is often outside our power. But what is within our power is our choice to love others. On the cross, hated and mocked, Jesus chose to say, "Father, forgive them, they know not what they do." He loved them. He showed us the Way. He provided an example of following the Buddha's advice: Focus on your ability to love, not your demand to receive it.

Choose kindness, choose love and unselfishness, choose faith, choose humility, even on death row, or in the hospital, or in a classroom, or out on the streets sleeping under a bridge. Very often our immediate environments or circumstances are not under our control, but our choice of Faith and Love always is under our control. We are not judged by what others do to us, but by how we respond. As a society, we will not be judged by how much crime there was, but by how we dealt with it.

Worldly Failure and Spiritual Success

Some of us consider our lives to be in one way or another, a failure. That means we are halfway there. We are the "poor in Spirit." *Blessed are the poor in Spirit, for theirs is the Kingdom of Heaven.*

Through the eyes of the Spirit, it is never too late to turn it around. And once we do, all those very things we considered to be our worst failures turn out to have been the very building blocks of our compassion and humility.

We have failed many times. We have let people down. We have been cowards, cheats, liars. We have hurt ourselves and others. If we allow our failures to open us up instead of shut us down, if we allow them to humble us instead of defeat us, then every destructive thing we have ever done can be turned into the very foundation of our devotion and compassion.

Do you "free-worlders" think you are better than a convict? Do you convicts think you are better than a snitch? Do you snitches think you are better than a baby-raper? Then you haven't failed enough yet. We are not better than anyone. That's the message. We have no right to look down on anyone, no matter what they have done. No matter what the world says or how the bumper sticker reads, pride is a vice, not a virtue.

Every human being contains the highest of the high and the lowest of the low. Often, we have to find it out the hard way. Sometimes we experience shame and humiliation. Such experiences bring us down from our lofty perch. It is important that during such times we do not quit or run away; that we do not try to forget all about it. We can accept our flawed nature, open our hearts and move forward quieter, gentler persons who know we are "just like all the rest." We can then become the peacemakers we all have the potential to become.

Putting Our Failures to Good Use

Without our failures, we may not have the credibility to help some of the youth, men or women on our cellblock, in our neighborhood, or in our classroom, to find a more decent way of life than guns, drugs, or deceit.

So, the question is, are we using our failures yet? Are we getting the spiritual point of our failures, and becoming transformed into a lifestyle devoted to faith and kindness and helping others? You and I deal with many people every day. Every one of those people hopes we are kind and humble and unselfish. They don't care where we learned it. They don't care whether it came easy or hard, or through failures or successes. If the building we are sitting in catches on fire, the people around us don't care where or how we developed courage; they just hope we've got it now so we can help them!

One thing we can begin taking for granted is that every person we meet who seems to have courage, dignity, compassion, and humility, has experienced failure and weakness and shame. We should not feel like we're the only one, or we're a worse one than the next. Everyone is connected. Everybody's in it together. Our personal and spiritual transformation rests only on what we are willing to do with it.

Faith and Failure

Maybe it seems that sometimes what starts out to be about faith leads into an experience of failure. But the two are not separate. Our death-row friend and the elderly lady with cancer express a type of faith which is tied to getting a particular result. Peter the Apostle had a faith that seemed to be as much in himself as in Christ. Both kinds of faith can lead us into failure because they are limited. We can then "lose our faith" as the elderly woman did, or we can allow that failure to lead us into a deeper, humbler faith as did Peter. The choice is in our hands.[5]

PRACTICE: Creating a New, Post-Littleton Civilization

This may sound like a tall order, or too far-fetched for a "practice." But in truth, creating a new civilization is what we do, like it or not, every day of our lives. For the past few hundred years we have been fascinated with machines and technology, and so that is the flavor of the new civilization we have created. It is an incredible success technologically, far beyond the wildest dreams of our ancestors who started down this path. New words and phrases for this new civilization have become common speech—radio, television, audio, digital, airplanes, computers, the Internet, cell phones, software, interactive, virtual reality, microwave, bits and bytes, silicon chips. The list could go on for volumes.

Tragically, this new civilization has spawned other words and phrases as well: generation gap, latchkey kids, assisted suicide, road rage, clinical depression, drive-by shootings, school shootings, super-max, post-traumatic stress disorder, prison-industrial complex, private prison, three-strikes, mandatory sentencing and many others. These are some of the new words involved with the human side rather than the technological side. As Jesus said, "Where your treasure is, there will your heart be also" (Matthew 6:21). We have treasured the high-tech side of life more than the human side, and so we have created a civilization where we can phone a friend from an airplane, while our children have become the most confused, angry and violent people on the face of the Earth.

As sad as the high school shootings were in Littleton, Colorado, it was equally sad—and frightening, too—to see our society's response. After the first week's ceaseless replays of interviews with survivors and victims' families, the second week's coverage focused on the question, "How can we prevent future Littletons?" The guest of choice was Janet Reno. Not Billy Graham. Not Mr. Rogers. Not the Dalai Lama. But Janet Reno, whose expertise consists of guns, police, courts, prisons, metal detectors. These are our *children* we are strategizing against, without considering that perhaps we need to bring the giant monster of high-tech civilization to a halt for a few days or weeks or months and ponder why so many of our children are going crazy.

One eighth-grade schoolteacher recently indicated that *one-half* of his students were on psychotropic medication—either Ritalin, Prozac, Lithium or something similar which children in other countries have never even heard of. This is not a minor blip on the screen. This is a problem of our civilization. A problem of how we spend our time, how we determine our priorities, how we see life's purpose. There are many people in the world who live in humble conditions and spend half their day just getting clean water, who are happier than we are and whose children are happier and more well-balanced than ours. Something is dramatically wrong with our civilization. Every day, each one of us either helps to maintain this dysfunctional civilization, or helps to create a new one.

Our own priorities will continue to create new civilizations, so if we are dissatisfied with the current state of affairs, we need to change our priorities. One of the Human Kindness staff members, Michael, often says, "Just pay attention to the inches, and the miles will add up." Creating a new civilization comes from creating a new day, a new hour, even a new moment. If you are a slave to consumerism and you waste time, energy and money on escapist activities, then you are going along just fine in the civilization which the corporate powers of the world hope to maintain. If you decide to step aside from the insanity today, and to focus your time, energy and money on kindness and good works, then you are joining many others in creating a new civilization which is not so anti-life.

One of the morning invocations in the Human Kindness community is, **"May my actions today reflect my deepest beliefs."** Another is, **"May our work and friendship today be of benefit to all beings."** We say these things and mean them, and try to hold ourselves accountable during the day. If our humanity does not soon catch up with our technology, we will be no more than a curious footnote in world history about a civilization which reached dizzying heights of gadgetry and then went mad before destroying itself. Please recognize Littleton for the serious wake-up call it is. Today, by your example, help to create a post-Littleton civilization which is happier and healthier. Dedicate your life today to the common good. Seriously begin to dismantle selfish priorities and replace them with nobler ones. We are responsible for civilization. Where our treasures are, there will our hearts be also.[6]

Simple Living, Simple Joy

We need to start asking ourselves some searching questions about why life seems to be of so little value to our kids. From a spiritual perspective, one sentence can sum up the whole thing: Human life is very deep, and our dominant modern lifestyle is not.

Our "task" is the spiritual journey and personal transformation. Life is deep, we are deep, and we're not acting like it. Life is inherently joyful, yet we're not enjoying it. We're caught in the details, in the "hundred other tasks" which will count for nothing if we don't wake up to our spiritual depth.

Right now, while you are reading this, take a moment to center yourself in your body, in this place you sit, and feel yourself breathing, and smile. Don't just speed-read on to the next paragraph, please. Let go of past and future. Appreciate that you're alive; appreciate knowing how to read. Appreciate knowing about spiritual wisdom. Bring a soft smile of gratitude into your heart and onto your face.

This is what we rarely pass on to our kids. Our kids don't get the message from us that being alive feels good. We may say it to them occasionally, but how do we *show* it in our everyday activities? Even the best, most loving people often seem to be working themselves into the ground, keeping up a frantic pace just to pay the bills and to keep resolving each day's repairs, breakdowns, details, and little crises.

Would YOU Want to Grow Up?

You must admit, from a kid's point of view, growing up doesn't look very appealing. Besides seeing so many joyless or angry adults in schools, businesses, and government, it also must appear that adults have little or no control over their lives. "Honey, I'd like to hang out with you, but I'm sorry, I really can't help it. I have to do such-and-such, I wish I didn't have to, but I do. . . ." How many times do our kids hear such words? What's the message they receive—that adult life, everyday life, is mostly a drag and out of control?

Everyday life is all we've got. The deep, wonderful secrets of life, the mysterious presence of the Divine, the joy of cherishing each other, the beauty of nature, the satisfaction of helping out, our journey into the ageless Wisdom—all exist *only* in our everyday life. There is no bigger ballfield on which to find Meaning. It's either right here, today, or it's nowhere.

Now, not after the revolution, not when our criminal justice system is improved, not when the next "Golden Age" brings worldwide peace and harmony. Here. Now. You. Me. Our kids. In the middle of the ghetto. In the middle of prison. In the middle of our endless details, our ceaseless worries about the future.

How many simple, peaceful, truly *happy* adults do our kids get to see? How many adults are deeply content with their lives and enjoy what they do? How many are happy about getting older, and unafraid of dying? How many are relaxed and calm, with time to play hooky from work every now and then in order to mentor a young person?

We seem to be knocking ourselves out in pursuit of a vague image of success and meaning, while the real quality of our everyday life with our families and communities steadily declines. We're asleep at the wheel, swept up in a fitful, agitated dream, and we're missing some gorgeous scenery that only passes by once.

When the Buddha experienced His great enlightenment, He got up from where He had been sitting and walked toward the village. The first person who saw Him was awestruck by His radiance and power. The man approached Him and said, "Sir, what *are* you? Are you a God?" The Buddha said, "No." The man said, "Well, are you a Spirit or a Demigod?" Again, the Buddha said, "no." "Are you a human being?" Once more, the Buddha said, "No." The man said, "Well what ARE you, then??" The Buddha replied, "I am awake." And then He spent the rest of His life making it clear to us that we can awaken too. The joy is right here; we just need to wake up to it.

The basics of life are no different today than they were thousands of years ago: Get up in the morning, take reasonable care of our bodies, minds, and souls; use your talent to do some kind of work that benefits the world instead of harms it; respect and cherish each other, and then get some sleep. It's important to keep our big view simple, and to pass such a simple view on to our youth. They need a Big View.

The Most Timely Activism

The most valuable form of activism in this day and age may be to explore a lifestyle based around simple living and simple joy. It may take toning down our materialistic demands and figuring out how to live on less income, but that process itself will begin to save some of the world's resources and thereby address many of the world's pressing problems, as well as giving us more time with our families and communities.

Many people think that they can't get by on less. But when we look around a typical suburban neighborhood of about 20 houses, and realized that there were 20 lawnmowers, 20 chainsaws, 15 rototillers, 10 table saws, and a lot of other expensive contraptions that each family may only use a few days each year. Among those 20 families there were about 45 cars, costing a fortune in insurance, repair, registration, gas, and so forth. Those 20 families owned probably 60 or more televisions.

When growing up in the 1950s, few families had a television. So people would gather at a neighbor's house to watch something—which, of course, provided natural opportunities to socialize with the neighbors. This still goes on in many other countries. But in our society, television has become the *opposite* force: Even poor families may have televisions in several rooms, so we hardly even socialize with our own families, let alone our neighbors.

This is a strong example that more is not always better. In cultures where people must share limited resources—televisions, power tools, vehicles—their sense of community is much stronger. We have bought into a model of progress and personal choice that has isolated us as individuals and actually damaged our family and community life a great deal. Is it really progress?

So these days, it is political activism to go against that tide. Share tools with our neighbors, cut down to one television in our home (and cut down our use of it greatly), eat meals with our families, go for walks, do daily readings of spiritual stories, occasionally play hooky together and go skip stones across a pond. It is activism to slow down and move through the day more gracefully; activism to explain to our kids the hype and deceit involved with the endless ads which incite them to buy something new or get in on the latest craze. Our children may be deeper if we treat them with depth. Our kids may be deeper if we are. No guarantees, but they'll certainly have a better chance. And it offers us the chance to become proactively involved in a profound form of preventive corrections.

The Big, Eternal Activism

Providing a *spiritual* perspective to our children is always the Big Activism. How many people proudly say, "I tell my kids they have to figure out whatever they want to believe in; that's their business?"

Why would be put such a burden on our children? We help them to walk, talk, ride a bike, drive a car. But not to teach them about their connection to the Great Wisdom handed down by so many elders and traditions? Not to teach them about the common threads of all religions? Not to acquaint them with the "One Task" in life which Rumi described—to be deep people?

It is sweetly ironic that the Great Activism of our day—inspiring our children to stay alive, and to live and behave in civilized ways—requires us to rediscover the simple joy of life for ourselves as well. We have to do it. Nothing less will do.[7]

PRACTICE: Mantras for Everyday Life

The Sanskrit word *mantra* is a combination of the words that mean "mind," "sound," and "protector." Mantra can be practiced on a couple of different levels: A person may take one of the names of God as a mantra, and try to repeat it silently throughout the day. Mantra steadies the mind. Over a long period of time, mantra can strengthen one's focus to an extraordinary degree. Mahatma Gandhi did the mantra "Ram" (God) for many years. When he was fatally shot point-blank by an assassin, the only thing he uttered as he crumpled to the ground was "Jai Ram" (hail God). No fear, anger, regret, just *Jai Ram*. Imagine such unshakable presence of mind.

We can also use mantras as a practical tool for reminding ourselves of changes we're trying to make in our lives. They can help us to break through old habit patterns and old, limited ways of seeing things. You may practice the following mantras in two parts: First, sit quietly with one of these in the morning and repeat it to yourself for at least fifteen minutes, letting the shades of meaning sink in deeper and deeper until you feel connected to what the mantra is saying to you personally. This is called "investing a mantra."

Step two, after having invested the mantra, bring it to mind as often as you can throughout the day, especially as you get caught up in the conflicts or busyness of what's going on around you. Let the mantra remind you of your deeper view, of your calmer core, of the depth you may have felt during the investment period. Let it help to change your view right in the middle of all the action. It will if you stick with it. Here are a few you can try:

Mantra: "It's Good To Be Alive"

To be alive, to be breathing, is good. *Before* anything is added that causes pleasure *or* pain, harmony *or* conflicts, comfort *or* fear, success *or* failure; *before* we are old or young, black or white, rich or poor, man or woman, imprisoned or free, **It's Good To Be Alive**. In and of itself. For itself. Don't overlook it. Be grateful. If you let that most basic appreciation slide from your awareness, you will be endlessly batted back and forth like a Ping-Pong ball between happiness and sadness, loss and gain, pleasure and pain, constant change. The most effective way to deal with the world is to be firmly centered in life's free, basic, unchanging goodness.

In the investment period, repeat **"It's Good To Be Alive,"** and gradually deepen your direct, gentle experience of being alive. Feel grateful. Bring a soft smile of wisdom into your heart to start the day, knowing that today will bring ups and downs like every other day, but you will try to not be a Ping-Pong ball.

Mantra: "No Hard Feelings"

This mantra has been powerful for a lot of people. During the investment period, as you repeat it to yourself, see how many different types of "hard feelings" come to mind. Let them all go. Even let your enemies off the hook. Soften and de-personalize such emotional states which have caused you nothing but pain for so many years. A related mantra is **"Nothing Personal."** When people try to exploit or harm you, scam you or humiliate you, it's not personal. It's their pain, their fear. Everyone is caught up in their own struggles; you just happen to be there, that's all. So if you use this mantra to remind yourself, at least all those encounters will be one-sided instead of your becoming an equal part of the mess. **Nothing personal. No hard feelings.** The more you see the truth of things, the easier it is to do whatever you need to do, but without self-righteousness, anger, bitterness. Every time you *feel* a harsh feeling, a hard edge, bring the mantra to mind. **No hard feelings.** It's tough sometimes, but it works.

Mantra: "Untouched"

During the investment period, while silently repeating **"Untouched,"** try to feel that part of you which has always been the same, through every experience of your life—that inner, unchanging witness of every moment. That is what is untouched. That is the One true, immortal Self. Take a few moments to realize that this Pure Awareness has been exactly the same during the best and worst events of your life. **Untouched.** Once you feel what I'm describing, even slightly, then the mantra will slowly strengthen your ability to rest in that Awareness as you watch yourself act and react in everyday life. It's quite a relief. And especially when you feel extremely caught, negative or frightened, the mantra **"Untouched"** can help you remember that it is only the character you are playing who is caught or frightened, not the Actor. The Actor, the Ancient One, Pure Awareness, remains **untouched**. This is a very good mantra for people who wish to be less touchy and temperamental. Your Real Self is beyond attack.[8]

Communion and Community

Religion was never supposed to be complicated, abstract, or distant from our daily life. In fact, both religion and philosophy arise from the *most* real, *most* practical questions of our existence: What are we doing here, and how can we make life work? Every thoughtful person, not just intellectuals or ministers, wrestles with those basic questions at some time or other.

For thousands of years, religions, philosophies, saints, and sages have tried to help us find the answers to those two simple questions. We have usually been content to argue and even kill each other over the *differences* in their teachings, but when we let go of such fearful separateness and look honestly at the *similarities* instead, we discover that the great "Wisdom Traditions" all point in *exactly* the same two directions: Inner transcendence (Communion), and unselfish behavior (Community).

What Are We Doing Here?

The ego is a monkey catapulting through the jungle:
Totally fascinated by the realm of the senses,
    it swings from one desire to the next,
    one conflict to the next,
    one self-centered idea to the next.
If you threaten it, it actually fears for its life.
Let this monkey go.
Let the senses go.
Let desires go.
Let conflicts go.
Let ideas go.
Let the fiction of life and death go.
Just remain in the center, watching.
And then forget that you are there.

                  – Lao Tzu

In response to the first question, "What are we doing here?," the Holy Ones have all said, (1) It's way beyond your understanding, so give up trying to figure it out with the mind; and (2) Look within, look *beyond* the mind, be STILL, go to the Secret Place within the heart. In other words, they point to an experience of direct contact with the Christ – Allah – Great Spirit – The Almighty-Yahweh – Buddha Mind, etc., which can only be found by going inside, past all our notions about self *or* God. Lao Tzu's poem sums it up perfectly: **Learn how to remain in the Center, watching—and then forget that you are there.** A word for this which no tradition would argue with is COMMUNION. The Great Religions and masters tell us to diligently seek Communion.

How Can We Make Life Work?

In response to the second question, the wisdom teachings, once again, have each expressed *exactly* the same advice, the same ethics and standards for human behavior: Be kind to one another; love thy neighbor as thyself; do unto others as you would have them do unto you; live for a mightier cause than selfishness; serve the poor; make the world a better place. Another simple, unarguable word sums it up: COMMUNITY. The Holy Ones all tell us to dedicate our lives to the Community. Lao Tzu says it in a way that gives us no excuses:

> The First practice is the practice of
> Undiscriminating Virtue:
> Care for those who are deserving.
> Also, and equally,
> Care for those who are not.
>   – Lao Tzu

Or, as Neem Karoli Baba put it more than 2,000 years later, Do whatever you must with people, but never shut anyone out of your *heart*, even for a moment. It's all the same teaching.

As Soon As . . .

It's easy to think of family and friends as "community," and everyone else as strangers, associates, rivals, or even enemies whom we just have to cope with in order to make a living, do our time, get ahead, etc. It's easy to think "I'll practice Community and Communion as soon as I get home from work, as soon as I get out of prison, as soon as my boss stops picking on me, as soon as things smooth out for me, as soon as, as soon as. . . ."

It just doesn't work that way. Our community is *exactly* where we are at every moment during the day; *exactly* whom life places in front of us at any time. That's the whole point! That idiot, that lecher, that bully, that pervert, that con, that cop, that snitch, that bureaucrat who drives us up the wall, that windbag politician on TV—everyone we see, hear, or meet must be respected as a brother or sister on the path, even if they have no idea there is such as thing as a path.

Clearly, this practice of Community is not for cowards; it's challenging and confusing, and it's full time. The world has become quite a mess from people only practicing it on the Sabbath, or in places where it's easy, or with people who are nice. We need some humble heroes who take it on full time. This means all of us. Now. *Today*.

Not as soon as, but now. Not when you get happier, but now. Not when people treat you more fairly, but now. Not when the world is a safer, kinder place. NOW. In the middle of the worst of it.

No one else in the world can play your unique role. God *knows* where you are, *knows* about your depression or anxiety, the people you face, your weaknesses, your past, your fears, and doubts. Communion and Community are not for later, they are your ticket out of Hell! If you decide to devote your inner life to Communion and your outer life to Community, that little suffering self doesn't have anywhere to exist!

Don't just say it or plan it; act on it today even in the *smallest* ways. If you are in prison, think about how long you have been there, and then ask yourself honestly whether the prison or anyone in it is better off because you have been there. Get to work. Make Communion and Community real. If you spend even a *moment* in humble silent reflection, if you help even one person or creature to feel safer or more loved, you will be on the road to the Great Recovery.

The Great Recovery

The Great Recovery is from the terrible addiction of self-centered living. That's the recovery all the prophets and sages have encouraged us to seek. Our whole modern world is hooked on looking out for number one, yet the more we do it, the worse we feel. So we up the dose of selfishness. It's classic addiction.

If the ancients are right—that Community and Communion are the only ways we're ever going to feel the joy of being alive, then imagine how it might feel if a whole nation lost touch with *both* Community *and* Communion. What would that be like? Well, as the late American sage Joseph Campbell said, "Just pick up the *New York Times* or turn on the television. We're *living* in what it would be like."

And it's pretty sad. Like the dogs at the race track who never get to catch the rabbit, not only do they not get to catch it, but it wasn't even a rabbit in the first place—just painted plywood! That's how we and our youth are getting ripped off daily by chasing after all the "stuff" that's supposed to make us happy but never will.

The only way we can restore Community and Communion in our society is first to restore it in our own lives: Just practice community in everything we do, and take time each day to seek communion beyond all names, forms, or identities.

Going It Alone

Few of us are ever in the ideal situation where everyone around us changes at the same time, or all the rules suddenly become fair. Most of the time we have to start this humble hero's journey by ourselves, with little or no support.

But then we receive the *invisible* support of Truth itself, because Community and Communion are a truer way than fear and selfishness. As Malcolm X discovered in prison, there is soul-power in taking a True Path. The harder it is, the more soul-power we gain. If it weren't so hard, we wouldn't gain so much commitment, courage, and faith. If it weren't so hard, Jesus, Mohammad, Moses, Buddha, and the rest would have preached to us from comfortable thrones instead of showing us the way through persecution, discomfort, rejection. It's hard because that's what it takes to move us beyond the ego; once we do, life isn't so hard anymore; even with all the same conditions in place, we find true peace and dignity.

Is There Truth In Our Goals?

Bo and Sita Lozoff have visited many treatment programs both in and outside of prisons. They have spoken to a lot of people who have been through the doors not just once, but two, three, four, five times—good people with decent hearts and a lot of sincerity, but who seem to keep finding themselves caught in addiction.

They ask why? Why can't I lead a good life? Why do I keep screwing everything up? I asked many of them what their treatment goals were, and received the same answer I've heard for more than 20 years: *"I just want to stay clean and sober, get a decent job, get back with my family, have a nice little place to live, a decent set of wheels . . . I'm a good person; I deserve it, don't I?"*

Those goals sound right, don't they? They would be applauded by television talk show audiences. But are they enough to create a happy life? "Me and mine" is basically what they amount to. "Me and my family." The practice of Community gets reduced to just a few people you love the most. And Communion gets shoved aside by the never-ending effort to catch all those plywood rabbits. Even if you're chasing them for your family and not yourself, they're still just plywood.

The *fascinating* thing is, if you investigate the anatomy of recovery failures—and most recidivism in general—you find two types—one which occurs during the first year, and the other between the second and third years.

The people who go back to using drugs (or other crime) during the first year seem to crumble because they fail to achieve one or more of those standard goals: Their spouse kicks them out, or they cannot find a decent job, etc., and they give up pretty quickly. It *seems* like an easy situation to understand: They didn't reach their goals, so they got discouraged and gave up.

But here's the fascinating part: The people who crumble between the second and third years, seem to fail *because* they reach the goals. Everyone has been there for them, gone out on a limb for them, they're loved and fed and employed . . . and that old constant craving begins again, and they keep it as a deep secret, until they are filled with shame and guilt, thinking "I must be a really horrible, ungrateful person to be craving drugs again after everyone has helped me so much; I must be rotten to the core." From there it's a pretty quick slide to "I may as well go ahead and get it over with; I'll never be any good, and they all may as well find out already."

The real tragedy is, they're not horrible people, they simply didn't understand that their "me and my family" goals were simply not big enough goals. They got what they wanted, and something inside was still empty and craving, because "me and mine" is not enough to make a whole, happy human being. Not wickedness, but simple ignorance was responsible for their failure. Has it happened to you, too? Will it happen next time?

Breathing Out, Breathing Out, Breathing Out...

We need to remember Communion as well as Community. Trying to dedicate yourself entirely through outward activity, no matter how much you seem to be helping others, will sooner or later chew you up and spit you out if you don't take time for inner silence. It's like trying to breathe out all the time without breathing in. How long can that last? Be sure you breathe in, too, so that you're helping others from a deeper place; a place where your personal transformation is expressed to others in ways that encourage where you live and work to become environments that cultivate peace.[13]

Questions

1. Do you feel it is important for each of us to make the "Big Change?" Why or why not?

2. Are many of us a little like "William" in that we find it hard to trust others? Do we sometimes feel like quitting and going back to old, destructive habits? Does our pride and resistance get in the way of learning what we need to learn in hard times? Is it important to "reach out" and "reach in" during such times?

3. What is the role of faith in the process of personal transformation? What is the difference between "blind" faith and a "dynamic" faith?

4. What do think about the "Sufi teaching story" on page 54? What is its relevance for us today?

5. Why is "communion and community" important? What are some ways you might practice this process?

Notes

The reader should note that this chapter is based upon an edited revision of editorials (with new material added) written by Bo Lozoff in *A Little Good News*, the newsletter of the Human Kindness Foundation.

[1] Canda, E.R. and L.D. Furman (1999). *Spiritual Diversity in Social Work Practice*. New York, NY: The Free Press.

Morgan, O.J. (2000). "Counseling and Spirituality." In Harold Hackney, *Practice Issues for the Beginning Counselor*. Boston, MA: Allyn and Bacon.

[2] Lozoff, Bo (1998). "Introduction." *A Little Good News*. Spring/Summer: pp. 1-2.

[3] _____ (1998). "Dying to Self." Christmas: pp. 1-2.

[4] _____ (1999). "When Everything Goes Wrong." Summer/Fall: pp. 1-2.

[5] _____ (1996). "Better Catch Up On Religious History"; It Doesn't Always End So Badly"; "God's Power, Our Power"; "Worldly Failure and Spiritual Success;" "Putting Failures to Good Use"; and "Faith and Failure." Christmas: pp. 1-3.

[6] _____ (1999). "Practice: Creating A New, Post-Littleton Civilization." Summer/Fall: p. 3.

[7] _____ (1996). "Simple Living, Simple Joy"; "Would You Want to Grow Up?"; "The Most Timely Activism"; "The Big Eternal Activism." Spring/Summer: pp. 1-3.

[8] _____ (1996). "Practice: Mantras for Everyday Life." Spring/Summer: p. 6.

[9] _____ (1995). "Communion and Community." Spring: pp. 1-3.

Law never made men a whit more just.
– Henry David Thoreau

. . . the delusion that a change in form is a change in substance.
– H.L. Mencken

*Idealistic reformers are dangerous because their idealism has no roots in love,
but is simply a hysterical and unbalanced rage for order amidst their own chaos.*
– William Irwin Thompson

Chapter 5

Transforming Institutions

Individual transformation is a necessary, but not sufficient step, in the development of a criminal justice system based on a peacemaking perspective. In a perfect world, all individuals would recognize the wisdom in treating others with respect, dignity, and concern. The move toward the transformation of all of us in this way is the work of the great religious and wisdom traditions of the world. As we enter the new millennium, this movement is still a work in progress. Although we hope that every individual will eventually find peace and justice in their hearts, in the meantime we must try to ensure that our social institutions encourage these objectives through both their expressed goals, and the means used to achieve those goals. In other words, our social institutions must model the very behaviors we are attempting to instill in ourselves. For some institutions, such as the family, the church, and the school, the principles of the peacemaking perspective are widely acknowledged as being desirable and effective. For other institutions, such as the criminal justice system, there is less consensus about the relevance of a peacemaking approach. In fact, a war-on-crime and a war-on-drugs atmosphere pervades the criminal justice system.[1] Any alternative to this war perspective is considered to be "soft on crime" and is easily dismissed by politicians who consider advocating peace and justice a form of political suicide.

In this chapter, we advance the idea that the criminal justice system is an appropriate forum to consider the peacemaking perspective. It is our contention that the more warlike the social institution, the more necessary is the peacemaking perspective. The more the institution deals with patriarchy, racism, and violence, the more it needs to demonstrate peace and social justice in its own practices. The criminal justice system provides a perfect occasion to illustrate how the peacemaking perspective can be utilized with the most disturbed, violent, and often most victimized members of society.

While the focus of the chapter is on corrections, we need to remember that the peacemaking perspective can be applied to the entire criminal justice system. The police and the courts are components of the system where peacemaking can be fruitfully employed in a variety of ways.[2] Some forms

71

of community policing and the practice of restorative justice are grounded in the peacemaking perspective. In addition, many law enforcement officers and other criminal justice practitioners routinely employ peacemaking techniques and philosophies in their daily endeavors. It should be acknowledged that while we focus on corrections, the peacemaking perspective is relevant for the entire criminal justice system.

In many ways, corrections has the most difficult mission in the criminal justice system. While apprehending offenders and dispensing justice are fraught with difficulty, there are some agreed-upon objectives, techniques, and practices that can serve as a guide. With corrections, the job is more difficult because of ambivalence concerning its mission. For some individuals, the correctional system is supposed to mete out the punishment handed down by the judge. For other individuals, the correctional system is supposed to demonstrate the folly of a criminal lifestyle so that potential offenders will be deterred from harming others. For still other individuals, the correctional system should reform the offenders so that they can become functioning members of society once again. And finally, many see the goal of corrections as repairing the social fabric of society that was damaged by the crime. This multiplicity of goals ensures that there will be debates about any particular correctional practice. Therefore, an underlying principle to guide correctional policy is needed. The peacemaking perspective is such a principle.

The Politics of Punishment

It is sometimes remarkable how we view punishment without a critical eye. It is as if we take for granted that punishment is the best and only method to correct inappropriate behavior. Parents spank their children; schools expel their students, and societies execute their criminals, all in a belief that visiting harm on the subject will ensure future good behavior and mete out a certain "just deserts" that demonstrates to all that no bad deed will go unpunished. These forms of institutional violence are accepted because of the intrinsic place punishment has in our society. Punishment is so pervasive that it is seldom examined for the destructive practice it so often can be. It is suggested here that punishment is employed by many because they actually believe it is a useful policy and that it is used by many others for many other ulterior reasons.

The first question we should ask about punishment is who profits from it? Directly or indirectly, there are a number of people whose careers, fortunes, or identities are bound up in the punishment business. We would be less than honest if we did not start our list with criminal justice professors. As part of a vast and growing criminal justice-industrial complex, we recognize that the academic field of criminology not only studies punishment, but does so in a way that often justifies and perpetuates its use.[3] The prison industry also benefits from our unexamined acceptance of punishment as a correctional practice. The growth in the number of prison beds for the past decade, even in the face of a declining crime rate, is evidence of prison systems as beneficiaries of a punishment response to crime.

A third party that benefits from punishment is the recently arrived private prison industry. The growing number of punishment-for-profit corporations have a clear interest in promoting a political and economic agenda that has punishment as its cornerstone. The media has also used crime and punishment as sensational items to boost ratings and sell newspapers. The media often presents a distorted image of crime and violence that gets translated into a fear of crime that is at odds with the actual level and severity of crime on the street.

Politicians use fear of crime to bolster their "tough" image and, all too often, pass draconian legislation that increases the level of punishment without regard to the cost or the feasibility. "Three-strikes" laws, mandatory minimum sentences, and charging children as adults are all practices that sound great on the campaign trail, but have little meaningful contribution to the criminal justice system other than to ruin lives and make incarceration more expensive. Politicians stumble over themselves to stake out a punishment position in their political agendas without regard to the actual causes of crime. They seek a panacea in punishment rather than dealing with racism, inequality, urban blight, unemployment, and other issues that require a political will. The short-sighted goal of getting elected forces politicians into positions that prevent them from taking a realistic look at the causes and solutions to crime. The pro-punishment stance that so many of them adopt is unfortunate and counterproductive as a crime control policy, and only adds to their constituents' and their own suffering. It is open to debate as to whether these politicians believe their tough-on-crime policies will actually work, or whether they are simply election rhetoric.

Finally, there is one more dimension of the politics of punishment that needs to be revealed. For many small towns, especially in rural areas, having a prison can mean the difference between economic survival and the death of the community. With a prison being the major, and sometimes only, industry in the area it has the capacity to transform not only economics, but also justice. Much like the company towns of the industrial age, the prison has a link to every family in town. Those who challenge the way the prison does business may find themselves and their families shut out of the economic and political mainstream. A scathing picture has been painted by Christian Parenti of Crescent City, California, where a new $227 million super-max prison is located.

> Many suspect that is exactly why the California Department of Corrections chose Crescent City: Economically weak regions often make gracious hosts for prisons. Hard times, it seems, also have a wonderful way of dulling empathy among the local citizenry. So willing has the town been to accommodate the prison that is seems like Crescent City has sold its sovereignty to the CDC. Today it is very much a company town, and discipline is its mono-crop.[4]

When the business of the town is the pain and suffering of the prison's inmates then the entire value system gets perverted. The prison world-view gets projected to the community's entire criminal justice system.

Making matters worse, the CDC pays fully 35 percent of the Del Norte County District Attorney's budget. Given these facts, it is hardly surprising that the citizen-jurors of Del Norte seem to hand out second and third strikes (i.e., life sentences) like lollipops at a bank. Thanks to the demonic economics of incarceration, those who enter Pelican Bay on small-time charges are often trapped permanently inside . . . For their willingness to destroy human lives, the citizens get to enjoy endless government cheese. It is in the town's interest to keep the prison horrific as well: The more inmates who go mad, the more "three strikes" dollars can be channeled north from Sacramento.[5]

With so many entities profiting from punishment, it is little wonder why it has become our policy of first choice. To look at alternatives requires that we step back and evaluate how effective punishment is at achieving the long-term goals of reducing crime and dispensing justice. Levels of crime are related to economic factors such as poverty and opportunity, as well as demographic factors such as the number of teenagers. Justice is a more subjective measure that requires looking at not only how street crime is treated but also how corporate and environmental crime is handled. In his book *The Rich Get Richer, The Poor Get Prison*, Jeffery Rieman provides a scathing account of how Lady Justice is not blind, but peeks at one's social-economic resources.[6] Despite our desires for equal justice under the law, the criminal justice system in the United States has a political dimension to it that often favors the wealthy and punishes the poor.

Any attempt to transform corrections into a more effective and humane institution requires us to become aware of the political and financial interests in the status quo. With the prison-industrial complex so entrenched in the opinion-making process, it is difficult to get a fair hearing for alternatives to punishment. Restorative justice measures and rehabilitative treatment suffer from being perceived as soft on crime and from challenging the vested interests of those who control the criminal justice system. We suggest that there are some issues and concerns that can make the correctional system more effective and can ensure that justice is better served, although these issues and concerns will typically be met with resistance. In evaluating this resistance, one must distinguish between vested interests and objective differences of opinion. The logic and eventual outcomes of the peacemaking perspective can overcome the skepticism of those who honestly doubt its relevance. However, the transformation of such doubters will require that they be convinced that their careers will not suffer as the process evolves from a punishment-centered institution to a justice-centered one.

In transforming the corrections system to a peacemaking perspective, there are a number of ideologies, policies, and practices that must change. The treatment of offenders as human beings who deserve respect and dignity is a hard sell in the criminal justice system. We are used to demonizing lawbreakers as being different from the rest of us and deserving of the most horrific punishments we can devise. It always seems politically correct to be prejudiced against, or even hate, inmates.

The history of punishment can be seen as a gradual process whereby the severity is reduced. At one time, the focus of punishment was on the body and terrible pain and suffering in the form of torture was considered the best way to deter lawbreakers. The emphasis shifted to incarceration where the soul became the object of focus.[7] The torture became less obvious, but the use of the dungeon has retained certain aspects of punishment that satisfies those who desire to see the offender suffer. While incarceration is clearly a better option than physical torture, it fails to make the offender less likely to commit future crimes, and it does a poor job of satisfying society's desire for harsh punishment. In the move to a peacemaking perspective, we will need to create ways of dealing with criminal offenders that can satisfy peoples' desires to see offenders pay or experience consequences for their crimes. It will be necessary eventually to recast the entire concept of justice from one of punishment to one of restorative justice. Citizens will always be frustrated with the criminal justice system that uses punishment as its primary goal. There is simply no way to satisfy the lust for punishment of someone who has had a family member murdered. The healing and recovery from such an event cannot be attained from watching someone else suffer. No matter how severe the punishment, the emptiness remains. What is needed is another way for healing the wounds of crime. Peacemaking criminology and restorative justice represent such a way. We present here just a few of the issues of the peacemaking perspective, and reserve for Chapter 8 a fuller explanation of restorative justice.

Opposition to Capital Punishment

Capital punishment is the most extreme correctional policy available in the United States. The taking of a human life by the government, in the name of justice, is a practice not used in other Western democracies. The United States stands alone in the community of similar countries in using the death penalty as a cornerstone of its criminal justice system. Even though the death penalty is not employed often, it has a powerful influence on public opinion and presumably on criminal behavior. It is assumed that those who commit murder will be faced with the prospect of losing their lives in the electric chair, by lethal injection, in a gas chamber, or some seldom-used method of execution. It is further assumed that this threat of capital punishment deters offenders from committing murder. We will not argue these points here for a number of reasons. First, it seems obvious that only a very few offenders actually get executed (although the number is increasing), so any expecta-tion on the part of the public that capital punishment is an effective punishment is not accurate. Second, offenders who commit murder often do so in the heat of passion and do not weigh the risks and consequences of their actions. Finally, and most importantly, even if the death penalty was used more often, and even if it proved to be an effective deterrent to crime, it still would not be consistent with the principles of the peacemaking perspective.

Figure 5.1
Peacemaking in Corrections

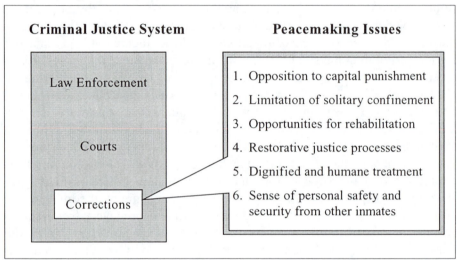

There are several significant issues concerning capital punishment, especially the way it is practiced in the United States, that make it unsuitable in peacemaking policy. Remembering the Peacemaking Pyramid Paradigm from the Chapter 3, it is useful to examine how capital punishment violates the concept of peacemaking criminology. The base of the pyramid is nonviolence.[8] Clearly, the execution of criminal offenders is a violent act. In looking at the history of the death penalty, we see recognition of this in the many attempts to lessen the violence used in executions. For instance, at some points in history, capital punishment was used as public spectacle, and violence on the condemned was the main attraction. During the Middle Ages it is reported:

> Some of these poor wretches were destined for executions that were entertainments in their own right, gaudy pageantries of violence and prolonged, agonizing death. In such instances, a formal parade, replete with dignitaries in full dress, would convey the condemned to the place of execution, often the town square. Feelings would run strong and find immediate, if generally restrained, expression. Amid the unfolding violence, the condemned prisoner had a script to follow. He was, for example, required by custom to forgive the executioner, who was considered God's agent.[9]

The violence of early executions included torture, mutilation, burning, the pouring of molten wax in the offender's wounds, and the flesh of his arms and legs torn with hot iron pincers. Modern executions do not use this level of public violence. The executions are hidden from citizens and are accomplished with bureaucratic efficiency designed to minimize the violence. The electric chair was touted as a painless method of execution, and, today, the same is alleged for lethal injection. In attempts to maintain public support for capital punishment, the government tries to make it more palatable by reducing and hiding the inherent violence in this premeditated taking of a human life. From a peacemaking perspective, there is no way to kill someone in a humane manner. The very act of killing constitutes violence.

The second principle of the peacemaking perspective is social justice. Here too, capital punishment as it is practiced in the United States fails. Critics of the death penalty point to the way it is imposed in a discriminatory manner.[10] Age, race, gender, and social class are all factors that influence who gets executed. Males who murder are more likely to be executed than females. Teenagers are less likely to be executed than older defendants (although this can be argued to be desirable and a planned legitimate form of discrimination). Rich individuals are rarely put to death by the state. And finally, the race of the defendant and, more importantly, the race of the victim, are factors used to decide who will get executed. The most likely death row inmate is a black male who murders an influential white victim. The way in which the death penalty is used in the United States reflects the overall inequalities of the society. From a peacemaking perspective, this disparity in who gets killed by the government is a social injustice that is intolerable.

Inclusion and correct means are the next two steps on the Peacemaking Pyramid Paradigm and do not pertain to the death penalty to the same degree as some of the other steps. The due process given to capital cases may vary across jurisdictions, but the extensive appeals process can compensate for this. Also, there is sometimes a disparity in the race of the defendant and the race of the judge and jury. Is it a trial by a jury of one's peers when the defendant is African-American and the jury is exclusively white? Given the history of lynching in the South, and other patterns of racial discrimination, the issues of inclusion and correct means can be raised legitimately when considering capital punishment.

The American court system is often confusing to all except those who work in it all the time.[11] The issue of ascertainable criteria is relevant to how the death penalty gets imposed because the defendant often does not understand what is being decided and how his decisions might impact on his case. While ascertainable criteria is a problem for the entire range of court cases, it is particularly important in capital punishment cases where a human life hangs in the balance between understanding and confusion.

The final step in the Peacemaking Pyramid Paradigm is based on Kant's concept of the "categorical imperative."[12] By this idea, Kant means, "Act only according to that maxim whereby you can at the same time will that it should become a universal law." Given the haphazard, arbitrary, and inconsistent way in which the death penalty is handed down in the United States, it is clear there is no categorical imperative operating. Furthermore, the idea that killing someone in the name of justice simply establishes the universal law that violence by the state is an appropriate response to the problems of violence by the citizens. Kant's concept clearly argues against capital punishment.

By applying capital punishment to the Peacemaking Pyramid Paradigm, we are able to see how the peacemaking perspective is at odds with the death penalty. At another, and more elementary level, this relationship should seem self-evident. The saying "Why do we kill people to teach people not to kill people?" has a certain ring of truth. The policy of capital punishment that is built on the goals of revenge and deterrence has proven not only to be ineffective and discriminatory, but it is also in direct conflict with the goals of the peacemaking perspective. As an institutional policy, the peacemaking perspective has the same goals as individual peacemaking. Healing and finding mutually supportive relationships work at both levels and killing by the individual or the state is forbidden. Taken to the extreme this proposition would mean the war would be immoral. The cases of the fleeing dangerous felon or self-defense would also be problematic. In an ideal world there would be no killing. However, this type of world is far in the future. The important point to remember, however, is that even the flawed world in which we now find ourselves, capital punishment should be inconsistent with the peacemaking perspective.

Opportunities for Rehabilitation

The dominant philosophy of corrections has shifted in the past 40 years from rehabilitation to punishment.[13] There are a number of reasons for this shift. There was little evidence that rehabilitation worked in any consistent way on the grand scale that behavioral scientists had proposed. Studies were mixed at best, and one survey of the available evaluations of correctional effectiveness concluded that while some programs worked with some offenders, no program worked for everyone. This survey was widely cited as evidence that "nothing works" even though that was not what it really concluded. Politicians and correctional officials jettisoned rehabilitative programs on the faith of this report despite counterclaims and experiences with inmates who benefitted from the opportunity to improve themselves while in prison.

Another reason for the demise of rehabilitation programs is the soaring prison populations. With the war on drugs came a crunch on prison space that saw states constructing new prisons at a feverish rate. Correctional budgets were devoted to housing and security with little left over for rehabilitative efforts. Inmates were warehoused with little support for their psychological and social needs. When these inmates were returned to society, they were less prepared than ever to live and work among free people. As a result, they were often bitter and violent. The resulting problems produced a recidivism rate that further reinforced the idea that rehabilitation didn't work. In truth, rehabilitation has not been given a fair trial in the court of public opinion. Its successes go unnoticed, and it gets blamed for many failures that it should not. Every time a released prisoner commits a high-profile crime, it is chalked up as another instance where rehabilitation failed even if the offender only sat in a prison cell and was not offered any opportunity to change.

Rehabilitation is also often viewed as being soft on crime. Instead it should be viewed as a way to protect society. Because almost all offenders eventually get released from prison, it should be the expressed goal of the correctional system to change the inmate's attitude, interpersonal skills, and vocational capabilities. If prisons release inmates who are full of hatred and bitterness, and are unable to get a job, the result will be predictable. The cycle of crime and violence will continue and there will be calls for even longer and harsher punishments.

What would an effective rehabilitation program look like? First, it must be voluntary. One of the criticisms of past programs is that inmates were forced to participate as part of the decision as to when they would be released. In the era of indeterminate sentencing, inmates were released when the parole board decided they were rehabilitated. This decision was based on whether the inmate completed a treatment plan. This mandatory treatment resulted in some inmates participating in rehabilitative programs simply to be paroled. They would do and say whatever was necessary to be considered rehabilitated with little regard for actually internalizing the treatment.[14] Therefore, in order to be effective, rehabilitation programs must be voluntary. Inmates can profitably use their time to learn new skills, correct drug and alcohol dependencies, and gain a positive sense of self in service to others by taking advantage of rehabilitative opportunities. Forcing them into programs as part of the release decision often ends up with rehabilitation being at the center of a game of subterfuge, deceit, and false appearances. Such a game is not what a peacemaking philosophy is based upon.

Treatment with Dignity

One of the more disturbing trends in corrections, from a peacemaking perspective, is the renaming of punishment as rehabilitation. If the intent of a program is to change the inmates' behavior, regardless of how draconian it may be, the program is called treatment. This extends even to such recognized punishment such as solitary confinement.[15] A more recent sleight-of-hand linguistic deception is the boot camp prison. Used with both juveniles and young adults, boot camp prisons are short-term (90 days) shock incarceration institutions designed to instill the virtues of discipline and self-esteem in young offenders. It can be argued that boot camp prison has positive features such as the short 90-day sentence that results in less opportunity for the negative effects of incarceration. Also, many boot camp prisons do have some education and rehabilitation components that might soften the prison experience. However, these positive aspects can be obtained without the military motif.

Boot camp prisons are based on the assumption that military basic training changes young people for the better and that the experience can be transferred to the prison setting with similar results. There are a number of problems with this assumption. Much of the credit that goes to basic training may belong to the entire military experience. The talent pool is different in military basic training and the boot camp prison. Recruits are screened to select those who would make the best soldiers while inmates are selected on who needs to be taken from society. Soldiers are not released into society as soon as they complete basic training, but rather, spend years in the military where their training is reinforced and rewarded. The goal of military basic training is to teach recruits to follow orders in a highly structured environment and on some occasions, to do what is difficult for most individuals: kill someone. The goal of rehabilitation is to equip the offenders with tools to make good decisions in an ambiguous environment where there is often very little structure. In short, military basic training aims to make good kids capable of doing bad things, while boot camp prisons aim to make bad kids capable of doing good things. To treat them in the same way is problematic.

Even though boot camp prisons may claim to instill values, discipline, and a sense of self-worth in offenders and that the experience will help keep them from returning to a life of crime, boot camp prisons are not really about rehabilitation at all. The appeal of boot camp prison is the cost. By having 90-day programs, the prison system can rotate four offenders through a prison bed each year. This is a quick and inexpensive way to handle a large caseload. In order to sell such short sentences to the public, however, it is necessary to convince people that this is a rigorous program and that offenders are being punished severely. The correctional system wants to have it both ways. They want the public to believe that boot camp prisons are a sufficient punishment for the crimes these inmates have committed. Also, the correctional system wants people to believe that the boot camp prisons actually do the offender some good.

Perhaps the boot camp prison idea would not be so bad if there were not some unintended byproducts that seem to go along with this type of correctional policy.[16] The first unintended consequence is the behavior that is modeled for the inmates. The humiliation and psychological domination these young offenders are subjected to is problematic for their future good behavior. The goal is not to get the offenders to charge a machine-gun nest, as in military basic training, but rather, to treat others with respect and dignity and not to beat or rob them. By subjecting the young offenders to the most demeaning interactions possible, we may be training them to bully, cajole, and mistreat others. Some observers of the boot camp prison concept suggest that it is best at developing new gang members and drug dealers.[17]

There is, finally, one more issue concerning boot camp prisons that is a problem from a peacemaking perspective. There is a very fine line between treatment and abuse in the boot camp perspective. The experience is supposed to be spartan, demanding, unpleasant, and challenging. When zealous staff push the offenders too far, disaster can strike. In a case in South Dakota, a young woman died of heat stroke after a 2.7-mile run. Staff members believed she was faking illness and allowed her to lie in the hot sun for three hours without treatment. One critic of the case said, " The danger in this is that you create notions that if you subject kids to brutalizing physical exercise, you change them. You create the notion in the staff's head that all you have to do is make the conditions miserable and anything goes."[18]

South Dakota is not alone in its concern about the methods and tactics used in its boot camps. Maryland's Governor ordered an investigation into continued reports of excessive force and child abuse in that state's boot camp prison. There have been reports of excessive use of force since the camps opened in 1996. The reports are becoming more frequent and may be a sign that the boot camp concept is evolving into an unreliable and abusive form of punishment. As boot camps move from being experiments and become institutionalized into the correctional system, it seems as if acceptable standards are becoming more difficult to maintain. This is often the case with innovative correctional practices that show promise in the developmental stages where the staff and offenders are carefully selected and trained. Expanding the idea to include more institutions with less competent and motivated personnel and a broader range of participants can reveal that the idea is not as innovative and effective as once thought. The boot camp prison practice that relies on stress, discipline, and punishment may be doomed to reflect even more problems and abuses as time goes on.

Relabeling abusive punishment as treatment, no matter how well-meaning, can not seriously be considered rehabilitation. There is a certain seductive logic that argues if the offenders can be cowed into good behavior and following orders while in the boot camp prison, they will have "learned a lesson" and will be better citizens when released into the free world. This logic is simplistic and misguided. It is easier to get someone's compliance when you control every aspect of their life. By putting them under extreme physical and mental pressure, they can be made to march in straight lines, run long distances, speak only when spoken to, and any number of other trivial and demeaning behaviors. To expect this conforming behavior to carry over into the outside world once the control is absent has proven to be an unrealistic expectation. Subjecting a youth to discipline is not equivalent to teaching him self-discipline. In fact, the intense discipline meted out in the boot camp prison experience may often be counterproductive. Boot camp prisons may be cheaper alternatives that satisfy some peoples' desire to get tough with offenders. Any claims about treatment are for the most part political rhetoric. In fact, two states, Georgia and Maryland, have recently decided to phase out their boot camp programs for juveniles.[19] Because of the lack of positive results and some cases of abuse, these states are either simply closing these institutions or converting them to treatment rather than military motifs.

Security from Other Inmates

One of the most unpleasant aspects of prison life is the company one is forced to keep. Being surrounded by a variety of individuals, including murderers, thieves, and rapists can be uncomfortable even for individuals who may have committed those crimes themselves. In his classic study of prison life written in the 1950s, Gresham Sykes included deprivation of security as one of the pains of imprisonment.[20] These pains of imprisonment are what define prison life and make it so unpleasant that additional punishment is not necessary to make prisons a place where inmates do not wish to remain or return. It is not surprising that on occasion inmates beat, rape, and kill each other. After all, that's why many of them are in prison. What should be of concern, however, is when prison staff, through their own actions or inaction, encourage such behaviors.

Using the threat of inmate violence is a powerful method for correctional officers to control inmates. Whether implicit or explicit, staff members may use the fact that there is always the fear that other inmates can gain access to each other. All it takes is for the correctional officer to make a mistake or simply turn his or her head. Once an inmate loses the confidence that the staff is doing its job conscientiously, the threat of inmate violence becomes a primary, defining feature of prison life. Put another way, using other inmates to enforce conformity to prison rules or allowing them to hurt each other because that's considered to be part of prison life, is dereliction of duty to the point of being criminal.

For example, Parenti reports that at the Pelican Bay super-max prison in California, guards would watch on video cameras as inmates fought.[21] They would place bets on which inmates would win in what they termed "roman games." These gladiator fights were a way to break the monotony for the guards. By simply allowing inmates from rival gangs in a small exercise yard at the same time, the guards were ensured of an entertaining fight. The inmates had little choice but to uphold the norms of gang life behind bars. Failure to fight would mean punishment by their own gang and the guards counted on this fact to provide them with entertainment. Our claim here is this is an extreme feature of prison life and not a regular one.

A more regular feature of prison life is the threat of rape. Whether the staff are responsible or not, the prospects of an inmate getting raped while in prison are substantial. Any attempt to estimate the number of rapes each year is futile. This is a crime that most offenders will not report because of fear of reprisals and embarrassment. Suffice it to say that rape in prison is a real threat and occurs too frequently.

Given the reality of prison rape, it seems reasonable to conclude that the criminal justice system is to some degree responsible. The threat and act of rape is a stable feature of prison life and one that the authorities are well aware of when they send someone to prison. James Gilligan argues that prison rape is part of the punishment intended by society.

> First, the relevant legal authorities, from the judges and prosecutors who send people to prison, to the prison officials who administer them, are all aware of the existence, the reality, and the near-universality of rape in prison. Indeed, this is one reason why so many conscientious judges are reluctant to send anyone to prison except when they feel compelled to, either by the violence of the crime or, as is increasingly true, by laws mandating prison sentences even for nonviolent crimes, such as drug offenses. Second, the conditions that stimulate such rapes (the enforced deprivations of other sources of self-esteem, respect, power, and sexual gratification) are consciously and deliberately imposed on the prison population by legal authorities. Third, all these authorities tacitly and knowingly tolerate this form of sexual violence, passively delegating to the dominant and more violent inmates the power and authority to deliver this form of punishment to the more submissive and nonviolent ones, so that the rapists in this situation are acting as the vicarious enforcers of a form of punishment that the legal system does not itself enforce formally or directly.[22]

Is this an overstatement? Do our criminal justice officials really intend homosexual rape to be part of the punishment when offenders are sentenced to prison? Certainly, most judges and prison administrators do not intend rape as part of the punishment, but the threat of violence is a concern that is well understood by all who work in the system and by the general public. Jokes about being put in a cell with a big guy named "Bubba" are commonplace when the prison is being discussed. The violence that happens in prison is, to a great extent, considered one of the primary features of deterrence.

Violence in prison is something that should be of greater concern to the justice system. From a peacemaking perspective, this threat of violence almost guarantees that incarceration will have no rehabilitative effect. Offenders will come out of prison bitter and more violent than when they went in. In addition to being schools of crime where offenders learn techniques of lawbreaking, prisons may also become universities of hate, where they learn the most extreme forms of antisocial behavior.

Peacemaking in Institutions

It is time that we rethink the purpose of our correctional institutions. The retribution and punishment goals that now dominate our thinking are proving to be ineffective and counterproductive to the overall goal of the protection of society. The brutalization that is done to inmates comes back to us in the form of violent crime and mental illness. Furthermore, the model of violence projected by the government with its "war on crime," seems to be mirrored by the citizens in more violence. On a more hopeful note, a federal corrections experiment in Texas is currently operating a prison based upon restorative justice principles. In addition, Cullen, Sundt, and Wozniak advocate a restorative rehabilitation model and suggest ". . . doing good is almost always preferable to the alternative—neglect or even worse, the conscious attempt to inflict pain."[23]

In this chapter, we have attempted to show how the peacemaking perspective is directly relevant to corrections. We have discussed how capital punishment and super maximum security prisons work against the reduction of violence in society. The goal of peacemaking and rehabilitation of the offender has been promoted as a legitimate and desirable correctional outcome. And finally, we have highlighted the problem of the correctional-industrial complex, where those who work in the criminal justice system may attempt to influence correctional practices to enhance their own careers.

Questions

1. Why does corrections have the most difficult mission in the criminal justice system? What could be done to make its mission less difficult? Does your solution(s) impinge on the rights of offenders and citizens and is it consistent with peacemaking principles?

2. This chapter argues that punishment is intertwined with politics. Critique that argument. Are politics and punishment inherently linked in a democratic society?

3. How does capital punishment fit in with the peacemaking perspective? Are there ever any legitimate reasons to employ the death penalty? Discuss how the death penalty is consistent or inconsistent with the major religious traditions; with your religious beliefs.

4. How would a peacemaking criminologist design a rehabilitation program for offenders? What principles of peacemaking would need to be addressed?

5. Violence between inmates is a constant problem in the contemporary prison. Do we have an obligation to protect inmates from each other or is the violence one of the features that make the threat of prison a deterrent?

Notes

[1]   Fuller, John (1998). *Criminal Justice: A Peacemaking Perspective.* Boston, MA: Allyn and Bacon.

[2]   Fuller, John. ibid.

3   Newman, Graham (1983). *Just and Painful: A Case for the Corporal Punishment of Criminals.* New York, NY: MacMillan. Additionally, criminal justice and psychology professors often make money as expert witnesses in criminal trials.

4   Parenti, Christian. *The Baffler.* No. 12, p. 121.

5   Parenti. ibid. p. 122.

6   Reiman, Jeffrey (1995). *The Rich Get Richer and the Poor Get Prison: Ideology, Class and Criminal Justice.* 4th ed. Boston, MA: Allyn and Bacon.

7   Foucault, Michel (1979). *Discipline and Punish: The Birth of the Prison.* New York, NY: Vintage.

8   Fuller, John (1998). *Criminal Justice: A Peacemaking Perspective.* Boston, MA: Allyn and Bacon.

9   Johnson, Robert (1998). *Death Work: A Study of the Modern Execution Process*, Second Edition. Belmont, CA: Wadsworth, p. 13.

10   Bohm, Robert (1999). *Deathquest: An Introduction to the Theory and Practice of Capital Punishment in the United States.* Cincinnati, OH: Anderson Publishing Co.

11   Blumberg, Abraham, S. (1989). "The Practice of Law as a Confidence Game: Organizational Co-optation of a Profession." In Sheldon Goldman and Austin Sarat (eds.) *American Court Systems: Readings in Judicial Behavior.* New York, NY: Longman.

12   Kant, Immanuel. "The Categorical Imperative." In Daryl Close and Nicholas Meier (eds.) *Morality in Criminal Justice: An Introduction to Ethics.* Belmont, CA: Wadsworth, pp. 45-50.

13   Palmer, Ted (1992). "Growth-Centered Intervention: An Overview of Changes in Recent Decades." *Federal Probation,* 56(1):62-67.

14   Irwin, John (1980). *Prisons in Turmoil.* Boston, MA: Little, Brown, and Co.

15   Jacobs, James B. (1977). *Stateville: The Penitentiary in Mass Society.* Chicago, IL: The University of Chicago Press.

16   Morash, Merry and Lila Rucker (1990). "A Critical Look at the Idea of Boot Camp as a Correctional Reform." *Crime & Delinquency,* 36(2):204-222.

17   Feeley, Malcolm and Jonathan Simon (1992). "The New Penology: Notes on the Emerging Strategy of Corrections and Its Implications." *Criminology* (30)4:449-474.

18   Gerrietts, Jennifer. "Death, Abuse at S. Dakota Boot Camp Prompt Scrutiny." Reuters. Dec. 4, 1999.

19   Associated Press. "Maryland Closes One Boot Camp for Juvenile Offenders, Demilitarizes Others." Dec. 12, 1999.

20   Sykes, Gresham (1958). *The Society of Captives.* Princeton, NJ: University of Princeton Press.

21   Parenti, Christian. *The Baffler* No. 12, p. 121.

22   Gilligan. ibid. pp. 165-166.

23   Cullen, Francis T., Sundt, Jody L. and John F. Wozniak. "The Virtuous Prison: Toward a Restorative Rehabilitation." In Henry N. Pontell and David Shichor (eds.) *Contemporary Issues in Crime and Criminal Justice: Essays in Honor of Gilbert Geis*, p. 29. Saddle River, NJ: Prentice Hall.

I imagine one of the reasons people cling to their hates so stubbornly is because they sense, once hate is gone, they will be forced to deal with pain.
– James Baldwin

There is a palace that opens only to tears.
– Zohar

You must go on, I can't go on, I'll go on.
– Samuel Beckett

Chapter 6

Letters from Prison

Life in prison includes a wide range of emotions, including fear, anger, despair, and hope. Within this broad context offenders and victims, family and friends, and prison workers are all affected in one way or another. Severe acts of violence and unimaginable expressions of compassion emerge through Bo Lozoff's correspondence with prisoners and all whom their lives touch.

Substance abuse, neglected and abused childhoods, self-centeredness, emotional and mental illness, and the isolation and hopelessness of most prison environments are explored as is the anguish of victims and their families and the difficulties faced by prison workers.

While the themes and emotions in this section are focused on issues related to prison, prisoners, and victims, they are issues with which we can all identify. We have all been confused and angry, betrayed someone else's trust and been betrayed ourselves, felt like giving up, and hoped for an answer to our suffering. As you read and reflect upon the correspondence, imagine that you are the letter writer. How would it feel to be that person? How could life have been different for them? What brought them to the place they are in? It may be too late for some, but is it? What would you do if you had the power to "correct" the offenders in question? How could such violence and suffering be prevented?

Expressions of Anger and Violence

Anger often justifies, in our own minds, the violence we inflict upon others. Sometimes the violence is physical while on other occasions, it is more psychological. Fear drives our anger which can be expressed through violent acts ranging from hurtful gossip to homicide.

"D"

Dear Bo,

Have you lost your goddamned mind! That candy-assed advice you gave "J" in our Christmas newsletter is Bullshit, man! I guess it may seem that I'm coming down on you. I cut for you. I really do. BUT, this man is 2 cells away from the guy who beat his MOMMA to fucking death with a god-damn baseball bat! He saw his momma's eyes roll to the back of her head.

Bo, Fuck it. This guy needs to get a shank and take this motherfucker off the count! Nobody on earth could live after taking my momma like that. I can practice spiritual principles later! As soon as they put that dude in the ground!

Bo, I'm not a killer. I'm so passive I make myself sick. Sometimes I'm FORCED into a fight, But I swear to God, that man would die if he did my mother.

This must be the ultimate spiritual challenge for this Brother ("J"). I wish I could talk to the dude. Ah hell, what do I know? I still think you're full of shit. I'll tell you what though, "J" has more guts than I do.

This is making me sick at my stomach, I'm fucking crying. Goddamn, but I'm mad! Man, I hope that nobody does that to my mom or dad. I'll kill em!

Later,
D

Dear D,

I appreciate the honesty and friendship in your letter. Yeah, it's intense, isn't it? Maybe more intense than any other situation we can imagine. You said, "I can practice spiritual principles later!," which of course, is our natural response when horrible things happen. We want to react from our gut. We don't want to think about right and wrong or anything deeper than "take this motherfucker off the count!" as you put it.

That's very natural. But it's also "natural" for a baby to crawl off a cliff or drown in a pool. Natural doesn't mean that it's good, or right.

One of the worst things a human being can do is to kill another human being on purpose—no matter who started it, what the circumstances were, whether there was any choice or not, etc. It's a tragic thing to do and has unpredictable consequences inside the mind and heart of the killer. It doesn't matter how natural it is or how much the victim "deserved" it. Look at the current popularity of executions. People are cheering outside the prisons, just like you may think you'd like to cheer if our friend from the last newsletter took out his mama's killer.

But murders and executions shame us all. It is the supreme failure of human conduct, the supreme failure of trying to be decent human beings. Our friend had the horrible misfortune to see his mama killed right in front of his eyes. It is not any sort of loyalty or love to respond "naturally" and become a killer himself. That's not what any mama wants for her son. Please think about this.

Spiritual principles are the most important, powerful tools human beings can use to protect ourselves from living like brute animals. They are especially important and powerful when things are at their most horrible. Look how Jesus made that very clear: He didn't say, "Father forgive them," over a little disrespect; He said it after being unjustly arrested, convicted, tortured and nailed to a cross! Spiritual practice is not about being "nice." There are heavy mysteries and secrets locked up inside of us. Spiritual principles and practices are the only way to unlock that Divine Nature in our hearts.

I gave our friend that "candy-assed advice" because I know his real nature, and I want more than anything else to help him experience that for himself. Life has handed him an incredibly intense challenge, and I want him to meet that challenge in the best way instead of the worst way. The best way honors his mother and makes her death mean something wonderful to the world. Your way would only continue the pain and bloodshed in a world which has quite enough already.

And remember, D: That guy "J" wrote to me. I didn't seek him out. He doesn't want to kill the other guy. Something inside of him has a deep instinct to go a different way. Try to have a little faith in whatever forces are at work inside of him. He's the one it happened to.

You're a good man, D, and I'm glad you felt close enough to me to speak your mind. This isn't an easy journey we're on together. But go back to my books and read them from a deeper place after all this, and try to understand that this stuff goes all the way, in every situation imaginable. No time out. The stakes are too high. The jackpot we're headed toward is better than your wildest dreams.

Love,
Bo

Dear Bo,

Thank you for writing back. I don't think the issue at hand has anything to do with that dude or revenge. Thank you for clearing that up. Love is the issue.

Revenge, crime, rent & food. It's all bullshit. It's just meaningless. It seems to me that what's important is that I treat you with dignity. I'm sorry that guy lost his mother. And to be honest, if it was MY mom, I'd kill her killer. Thus becoming the killer! I don't even want to be able to respond any other way.

However, I believe I was wrong. You made the point: "that guy wrote me." You're absolutely right. The fact that he has even CONSIDERED an alternative means he is so much more spiritually advanced than I can hope to become. I honor him, if I may.

I was angry. I wrote that letter before I even finished the entire newsletter. You say honesty & friendship in that letter. I don't know what my motive

*for writing was, maybe trying to get a personal letter from you! I do oper-
ate that way. But my letter was spurred on by anger. We know anger is only
fear.*

*God wants warriors not cowards. It's easy to be a coward. But it's hard
to stand up for what's right. ". . . this stuff goes all the way, in every situations imaginable."*

*I guess I'll close, Bo. I'm so proud and puffed up that you're where you're
at spiritually! I'm even more glad that I'm part of it. I hope the universe does-
n't get together and humble me. I hate it when that happens. Thanks again
for writing to me. Thanks for YOUR honesty and friendship.*

Respectfully,
D

Lloyd

Dear Bo,

*I hope this letter finds you exceptionally fine. A lot has happened in my
life since I last wrote you. I decided to cut my own foot to get into the hospital. When I cut it I went in at the bottom of my foot in which now I'll never
be able to run again.*

*Also I got hooked up on a "battery on another inmate" charge. This dude
who was involved in the death of my partner came here, and I couldn't back
off from trying to take him out after I heard him bragging about it. I took an
iron leg of a chair and walked up behind him while he was playing cards and
tried to knock his brains out, but it only knocked him out and put him in a
coma. I was locked up and now am on maximum-security lockdown.*

*I don't have any regrets at trying to kill him and even if he died and I
received a life sentence, I still would not regret it. I know you feel I'm
wrong, but I respected my partner and I's friendship to the extent that I felt
what I did had to be done. I'm old-fashioned when it comes to values and
morals and living by the convict code, but that's me, and I've never claimed
to be anyone but.*

In eternal friendship,
Lloyd/La.

Dear Lloyd,

I hope you meant it about "eternal friendship," because I'm going to be
straight with you. Sounds like you're snowing yourself, my friend. You're picking an argument with me over what you did, when I haven't judged you in the
first place. I think you're arguing with yourself, and laying it off on me.

I'll play along; I'll answer as that part of yourself that wants to argue
about what you did. You talk about the convict code, but that's bullshit. There's
a higher code that we all answer to, and it says that when we purposely bring

more suffering into the world, our own lives will suffer as well. The guy you offed brought suffering to your partner. Now you've brought suffering to him. Next maybe a friend of his will hear about it and come looking for you. And then a friend of yours . . . You know, with good "old-fashioned" convicts like you around, the state hardly needs the death penalty!

You knew what this letter would be like before I wrote it, because it's coming from the part of you that has been hip to the stuff we've been sending you through the years. I appreciate how much it hurts to feel the death of a friend, and especially to hear someone bragging about it. And I'm not even saying you shouldn't have done what you did. All I'm saying is cut the shit, and face up to exactly what it was: A self-destructive, spiritually uncool act that came out of attachment and anger. It had nothing to do with living up to codes or moral values.

In view of what you did to your own foot, too, it's got to be getting obvious that you're way out of tune with your own happiness right now. So stop making excuses and inventing philosophies, and start thinking about whatever you need to do to come back into the center of the picture. Since you're in the hole now, maybe you can use some of this time to pray for help, and get back into meditation and that sort of thing.

You can't undo anything you've done; none of us can. But you can start taking honest control of your life again and open yourself up to the deeper, higher realities which can help you get your head straight. Life is really much bigger than you've been allowing yourself to experience. Did you think all this spiritual stuff is just a bunch of poetic words and high-sounding nonsense? It's a lot more real and powerful than the convict code!

> Come on back, brother,
> Bo

Tommy

Dear Friends,

I'm searching for my spiritual awakening that so far I've not been able to find, but my life has come to a point where I need to find myself before I'm lost in the terrible maze of unknowing.

Let me take a few minutes to tell you a little about myself and my present situation. Hopefully it will help you to know what it is I'm trying to find. I'm 27 years old, born Sept. 9, 1950. I'm presently in the Idaho State Prison for first-degree murder, two counts. I was sentenced to death in March 1976, but the Idaho Supreme Court vacated my death penalty.* These two charges in Idaho aren't the only ones I have. There are seven more in other states. Please let me explain why I did these cold-blooded, without any mercy, killings.

In April of 1974, eleven men entered my home in Portland, Oregon, raped my 17-year-old wife, who was three months pregnant at the time, then threw her four stories out our apartment window.

You see, I had been running drugs and guns for some people out of Nevada. My wife had asked me to stop so I tried to get out but they said no. On my next run I kept the goods I was to deliver and told them I'd turn it over to the feds if they tried causing me any trouble. I never would have, but they thought I was serious. Well, they set me up on a phony bust to get me out of the way thinking I had told my wife where I had stashed the stuff. I never did!

So, when they went to our house, after beating her and realizing she really didn't know where I put the stuff, they gang-raped her and threw her out the window. By some freak accident she lived for several months after that, long enough to tell me who most of the eleven were. She committed suicide while in a state mental institution, as her body was so crippled up from the fall, she had lost all hope and just wanted to die. In August of 1974, I went after the eleven guys who did it and caught nine of them in several different states. I was unable to complete my death mission and get the last two because I got caught here in Idaho.

Since all of this happened, I've had no inner peace at all. All I can think of is my wife, the only person who ever loved me and all I had in this world. I can see the men I killed and the look of pure fear and disbelief that I'd found them, as I took their lives. I'm not saying I was right for what I did, and I can't really say I'm sorry. I only know that I have no peace, happiness, or love, but at times I feel that I can have, but I just don't know where to look. I need help but I have nobody to turn to. My family has turned from me and I have nobody to write to or to visit me. I can't carry my burden alone anymore, so I ask you from the deepest of my heart, please send me any material that you think might help me. I am in maximum-security solitary confinement and have been for almost four years.

Really, all I want to do is find that something that I know for a fact exists that will free me from all my burdens. I would appreciate any correspondence that can help me find my way to a new and better life. Thank you for your time. Please reply!

Sincerely yours,
Tommy/Idaho

*Tommy's death penalty has been reinstated, and at this time (1985) he's back on death row.

Dear Tommy,

Your letter has touched me and Sita deeply. We're happy to know you. In one sense, you've got an unusual story; yet in another sense, you're in exactly the same place we all are: Simply a person who's waking up to the journey, and wondering what you can do to get on with it. As heavy and fierce as your own life has been, it's not the details so much that matter once we start this process of awakening.

It's true that every thought, word and deed counts. But it's also true that the journey is a much bigger one than most people imagine. And in the course of all that time, it's possible that each one of us has to pass through the very gates of hell and madness like you, your wife, and her attackers did during the past few years.

I don't mean to imply that you should look back and feel good about it, but just to try to understand that no accidents happen in this universe. Even the most horrible experiences can still be steps along the way. And the pain which may still lie before you as a consequence of killing nine people—just more of the same: difficult, necessary steps on your path.

This understanding is the beginning of true faith. My faith first woke up when I was 18 and I drove head-on into a tractor-trailer at close to 100 mph. I was a bodybuilder at the time. My whole life was based on body stuff, and suddenly I'd never be able to do any of that again. I had permanent injuries; I could bitch about them, but they were what they were regardless.

The same thing happened to me as is happening to you: I knew there had to be something, some way of looking at my life, that could open the door back up to the possibility of happiness. In your case, the "permanent injuries" are the fact that you'll probably never see the streets again in this lifetime. That's a fact you need to face in order to plan a strategy for your life.

A good first step is to begin quieting the mind, and this is what all our meditation materials are about. All the answers, all the guidance you ever need, is already within you, but the noisy mind can't figure out how to tune into it. What I mean by noise is stuff like desire, fear, guilt, self-pity, anger, hatred, pride, pettiness and so forth. The way most of us grow up, our lives are pretty much a confusing combination of such noise from the time we get up in the morning until we fall asleep exhausted each night. No wonder we're so tired!

But meditation practices, especially with the kind of time you're doing, can be your gateway into the deeper realities of life, the deeper parts of yourself; which can help you go through your pain rather than trying in vain to go around it.

It's not going to be fun or easy. Meditation is always pretty hard, and when you may be opening into intense guilt or grief, it's harder still. The only thing harder would be to try to ignore it all, and live an empty life feeling alone and isolated. It's more a matter of facing whatever experiences your life brings you and using them to become free.

Of course, all of this is much easier said than done, I know. I know you've been through terrible pain. I'm just trying to help, and I figure if I throw about a million words at you, maybe three or four will hit home. At least you can count on having a family again. Much Light for your day,

Love,
Bo

Dear Bo,

I just received your most beautiful and encouraging letter and I was so happy to hear from you. Thank you so very much!

I'm not always an emotional person as far as letting my feelings show, as my past lifestyle required that I never let nobody get close or at no time let anyone know what I was feeling at any time. But in these past few weeks since I first read INSIDE-OUT, I've been becoming aware of myself and of other people more each day, and I've been experiencing feelings that I had all but forgotten. Then today when I got your letter and the books, something happened to me that I never would have dreamed possible.

Since that first day I picked up a half-torn copy of INSIDE-OUT and began to read it, I felt that at last I had found what it was I had been look-ing for all my life. And something told me to write and find out more of what this had to offer me in my search for spiritual awakening. At first I was pret-ty skeptical because I had been through so many other trips, and had been let down so many times. But something kept telling me not to just read this to help pass the hours away but to read it and keep it in my heart and mind. So, each day I've been applying some of the things that I've read to my daily life, and I've been like a new person.

When I got your letter today, I noticed my hands were shaking as I was taking it out of the envelope. Well, as I started to read I felt a warmth come over me as I have never felt before, and a voice within stilled my fears and seemed to say that at last you're coming home and you have no need to fear ever again. As I read on I noticed that I kept having trouble seeing and my face felt like it was on fire. So I reached up and started to rub my eyes and it was only then that I realized that I had tears in my eyes and running down my face. Then they came freely as I knelt to thank God for that little book and for you and all the others that are trying to bring the world together to live in harmony with each other and with God.

It has been a long time since I was able to let my heart open up and let myself really be free and feel again. What can I say except, I thank you and you have my undying gratitude and friendship. Not only because you have come into my life and touched me, for the many others that I know you have touched and helped to find that wonderful road to a new and better life, the only life! Thanks, Bo, for the letter and for sharing part of your life with me. May God give me the strength, faith and courage to continue on this jour-ney that I have been fortunate enough to find. Now I'm happy again and it's been a long time, but it sure feels good . . .

I enclose a couple of poems for you and hope you enjoy them. Please feel free to use my letters or poems in any way that you feel might help others. I'm not ashamed to tell the whole world that I have found a new life. I see a lot of chances in my life already from my daily meditation practice; it's working wonders, and I seem to be getting closer to people already.

With Love and respect, your friend and Brother,
Tommy

Questions

1. "D," Lloyd, and Tommy all seemed to be motivated by getting payback or revenge; "D" reacting hypothetically to what he perceived as "candy-ass" advice Bo gave another inmate concerning his mother's murderer residing two cells away from him; Lloyd for upholding the "convict code" in trying to kill the killer of his partner; and Tommy for killing nine of the 11 men who raped and tried to kill his wife, who later committed suicide. How would you feel if you were these men?

2. How would you feel if your mother, husband, wife, or close friend were murdered by someone and you knew where they lived? What would you want to do? If you reacted as these three men did (or wanted to do), what do you think the consequences should be? Why is it important that "D," Lloyd, and Tommy learn how to be calm and clear through mediation, prayer, or some other related practice?

"H"

Dear Bo,

If a loved one or a family member were murdered, what would the murderer have to do to receive your forgiveness? Guilt has led me to take charge of my life and make changes of my life and make changes that are improving my standards, beliefs and values while simultaneously helping others do the same.

I am withdrawing the appeals from my homicide conviction and pleading guilty. The changes in my life have guided me in positive directions and I accept responsibility for my actions.

I want to share the truth with the victim's family. I want to apologize, ask for forgiveness and give them the opportunity to express their feelings. I think and hope that this will help the victim's family to relieve some of the pain and suffering that I have caused.

The victim and his family were friends of mine before the incident occurred. We both had a bad reputation for shooting anybody who would get in our way. I did not intend to take his life.

I admit that it was my actions that caused his death. I know that I can't bring the victim back to life, but I will continue to work hard on improving my standards, beliefs and values so that I can be the son his mother would have wanted her son to be. I will also share these experiences with others so that they don't do the things I did. Forgiveness is a healing process. How can we ask God for forgiveness if we can't forgive each other?

I would also appreciate all and any information you might have that will help with my project. Thank you very much . . . Your answer will be of great value to me and to others.

Respectfully yours,
H.

Dear H,

There is no way to guarantee that a victim's family will ever forgive you for the pain you have caused them. That is up to them, and it would in fact be selfish on your part to keep struggling to gain their forgiveness. The last think you want to do is upset them more, so after an initial contact—letter of deep apology, remorse, etc.—I think it's proper to back off and let the next step be up to them.

One very practical way you can help them is to pray for them every day—not just for their forgiveness, which is still about you; but rather praying for their peace and their healing even if they need to hate you forever. You have to make this be about them, not about yourself. That's the key.

And of course, the lifelong payback on your part is the same whether they respond to you or not: To become a deep, caring, unselfish person who tries to help instead of harm. You owe that debt to the whole world, not just your victim's family.

Having committed murder can humble you forever; the world needs humble people. Having been so selfish can inspire you to be unselfish from now on. The world needs unselfish people. Give yourself to the world. Care for whomever life places in front of you at every moment. Let this whole experience quiet you and deepen you so that you are not a loud, pushy, petty, or greedy person.

That's as much as you can do. And it's enough. Your heart will heal, and as it does you will find it easier to allow your victim's family to heal in their own way, in their own time, without wanting to push them to do it for your needs. Hope this has helped give you some things to think about.

You're off to a good start,
Bo

Questions

1. What about "H's" desire to seek forgiveness from the family whose son he killed? Is there any way he can repay the debt of taking their son from them?

2. How would you feel if you were a member of the victim's family?

3. What was distinctive about Bo's suggestion that "H" pray for them?

Maury

Maury Logue, #89201 at the Oklahoma State Penitentiary, was a very bright guy and a gifted artist. He was also considered one of the most dangerous convicts in the country. He had stabbed so many other inmates that he was on 24-hour lockup and was handcuffed even to be led to shower three times a week. He's been on lockup longer than any other convict in Oklahoma, with no end in sight.

We first heard from Maury around 1975. He wrote intelligent, gentle letters and sent us some of his artwork. At some point over the next four years, a terrible bitterness ate into Maury's heart like sulfuric acid, burning a deep, smoking hole that was more painful than he could bear. Because of his violence over the past few years, Maury had so much time piled on top of his original sentence, he did not expect to ever see the streets again – unless he escaped.

Writing letters of encouragement to Maury, I had to keep in mind that he spent every day of his life in a cell smaller than my bathroom, surrounded by people who fear and hate him. I had to remember that the only human touch he ever experienced were the hands which cuffed his own.

I had no interest in helping Maury to "cope" or play mind games with himself in order to survive. I saw myself as his second in a duel; just holding his cloak, reminding him of his truest weapons, and wondering, with a good deal of awe, just how well I would fare on the same field of battle.

Here is a taste of our correspondence. This correspondence began in 1979, with Maury's first written description of his vicious transformation.

Dear Bo,

Since as far as I know—you and your family are the only people on Earth who sincerely care for the people, the poor people who are confined in teeny tiny cages like animals; it is to you, I wish to pour out "some" of my pent-up feelings concerning society in general.

I stole $25 in an unarmed robbery, I was later apprehended, and sentenced to 25 years in a rusted-out cage . . . simply to "rehabilitate" me (according to the prison authorities). Society supports these cages which house only indigent people! Society is a malevolent mass of morons as far as I'm concerned! I have a friend in here who got drunk one night, thrown in a jail cage, and ended up kicking the toilet off the wall. The courts sentenced him to 12 years in a cage . . .to "rehabilitate" him! At $10,000 per year, per prisoner, that toilet will cost $120,000 . . .think of all the poor people that money could feed! The state is willing to waste $120,000 to get revenge on a drunk for destroyin' a stinkin' toilet! You see in Oklahoma a toilet is held in higher esteem than 12 years of a man's life! In a materialistic country like America it's considered a terrible thing to steal money, but it's okay to put poor people in cages and leave them there until they go mad, and then release them on society.

I was a robber when I entered prison, and now after only four years of being "rehabilitated," in a cage, I am contemplating becoming a sniper when released. Society has gotten its revenge on me . . . they've shown me revenge is the righteous, holy way . . . that the only way to "rehabilitate" people is to punish, punish, punish! So after completing a four year course in "rehabilitation" I want to spread this "divine rehabilitation" to our wonderful society! Yes . . . just as the authorities have attempted to ameliorate me by punishment . . . so in like manner, I do wish to ameliorate society by punishment! I have reached the inevitable conclusion that society is insane! They MUST BE EXTERMINATED, beginning with the "leaders."

Now, I can't afford to purchase cages to put society in like they do the poor . . . instead, I can only afford a high-powered rifle with a scope. I will simply blow the tops of their skulls off . . . it will be quick and efficient, and it will have an auspicious deterrent effect on all aspiring lawyers, judges, d.a.'s, and politicians.

Perhaps you might even think I'm just "talking," I can assure I intend to do everything I've said I would, and then some!

I love speaking to you, Bo, for you listen, and you don't go for the lie that society does, that they're too pure, too innocent to associate with us "bad ones." The only thing that separates convicts from society is the fact that the convicts got caught! Society . . . there's not a single one of those pompous assholes that haven't broken a law or two. Not a one of them are innocent!

Hey, the authorities "blew" $40,000 tax dollars to convert a small-time robber into a big-time sniper! (me). I'm soooo very grateful for all the "rehabilitation" they've given me to make this possible! Will the joys of incarceration never cease?

Luv,
Maury

Dear Maury,

Sounds like heavy times for you. I really hope you're feeling better than when you wrote. Getting out and killing people is quite a bit different from the kinds of things we seem to have had in common so far. I mean, what is it about my family that you love so much? Whatever you admire and respect in us also exists in you. If you love it in us, then you'd like to be that way too.

Your anger and bitterness are excess baggage that you can no longer afford to lug around with you. I really do understand your pain and anger, and wanting revenge on those people who have made your life so miserable. But if you go kill a few people, then those people will simply check out of this life and take birth again too. The world will go on much the same as before, with a little more suffering, rather than any less. And then you're born into that world of greater suffering, which means you may have it even tougher than you did this time; and maybe you go to prison again, and get out again, and kill some more people, and get killed again, and take another birth, and suffer more . . . Maury, aren't you tired of it yet?

There's really no such thing as "society." There's a bunch of scared, lonely people who seem like an organized society, but we're not. And you and I are as much a part of it all as anyone else. So if you're going to start shooting, you may as well shoot me, Sita and Laxmana first.

We're friends, and to me that means we don't have to pull any punches with each other. Take the luxury of being absolutely straight with me, and know that nothing you say or do will change my love for you. You're my brother, even if I think you're full of shit.

Love,
Bo

Dear Bo,

Thank you, dear friend, for taking the time to write me. As for my aspirations of becoming a proficient sniper: You seem to have misunderstood my motive . . . you seem to think I'm "vindictive." On the contrary, I want to repay society for all the "kindness," "compassion," and "obvious concern" they've shown me. I want to "help" them; do you see?

You're wrong in your assumption that the world will go on much the same as before; after I pick off a myriad of "leaders." For it will start a "fad." America will be like Italy . . . there are many anarchists in America waiting for someone to kick it all off. I shall be that one.

You're wrong again in your assumption I might be slain and have to reincarnate in this miserable terrestrial realm. By your philosophy I can tell you're familiar with the Bhagavad Gita . . . Well, in it there is such a thing as karma—action without fruitive reaction! It's when you are in KRSNA consciousness, which is exactly what I'm in!

Bo, why don't you "help me," to "help society?" Take a gun, pick out your "friendly" neighborhood district attorney, or judge, and simply exterminate the ugly body that confines his wretched, unclean soul? DO YOU WISH TO HELP?? REALLY HELP?? THEN DO IT???

Luv, the "rehabilitated one,"
Maury

P.S. Definition of a politician—that's a person who's got what it takes, to take what you got!

Dear Maury,

Sorry, but I just can't buy your trip about wanting to kill people. First of all, you and I are very far from being in the state of "Krishna Consciousness." That's the same as being in Christ consciousness; it's a state of pure Love, a love so profound and intense that you see beauty in everyone and everything. Maury, you're angry and bitter and hurt, and your own hatred is driving you up the wall. You could kill everyone in the world, and you'd still be sitting there the biggest loser of all, because you have no peace.

You don't have to keep explaining to me how unjust and unfair society is; I know all about that, I assure you. Meanwhile, when you really come to understand karma you'll see that no one ever gets away with anything. Everyone pays for their unkindness and unfairness, and you don't have to be the fool who delivers their punishment. That's just more karma for you.

I know they've done awful things to you, Maury; I really do. And if you just want to strike back in some way, of course there's nothing I can do to stop you. But let's cut out the bullshit about it being spiritual or holy, all right? Bitterness and revenge are not going to get you closer to God. It just makes you more like the people you hate.

When are you going to let it sink in that what I tell you is for your sake, not for the sake of the people you hate? I'm not defending anyone's actions or misdeeds; I'm just trying to help out a brother who's in an incredible amount of pain. All this stuff about love and peace are not just head-trips for goody-goodies. It's the heaviest, most revolutionary message in town, only for super-strong dudes who see that they can't let other people's trips drive them crazy. So far, you're just not as strong as you want to be. And you know it.

I love you,
Bo

Dear Bo,

If you think I'm one of those "phonies" who just talk big—all you need to do is examine my prison records and mental asylum records. Since the last time I wrote you, I've stabbed three reprobates, beaten a myriad of others, and put several on protective custody. I don't like fools, I have no patience or sympathy for them. I haven't actually killed anyone yet, but it's only been because I was drug off before I finished the job. All my life fools have provoked me. I'm quiet, introverted, and a curiosity to them. Thus, they seek to "test" me. They only need test my mettle ONE time and they will immediately realize they made a fatal mistake!

I meet their arrogant, bold, stupid, otiose threats with a smile cold as ice. And when the doors open to the cages I'll still be smiling as I stroll into their cage with a nice long razor-sharp knife. I grin all the way through the stabbing . . . their screams are music to my ears! The horror on their faces is testimony to their newfound respect for me. I experience no remorse in eliminating human pests.

It's a law of the jungle! Only the craftiest, toughest, most dangerous of men is treated with the deference he rightly deserves. Not only did my dad beat me as a child, bu so did groups of older boys. Since I've been in here, eight big guards (good squad), armed with clubs the size of baseball bats, attacked me in my cage. I hurt three of them, and knocked two completely out of my cage. One was knocked out and quit his job. I eventually was "subdued" . . . and naturally beaten and scarred for life. After my arms were cuffed behind my back and legs shackled, I was beaten and kicked again. I was

bruised from head to toe. Do you think that will change my mind about exter-
minating as many advocates of prison that I possibly can!?!
    No mercy offered, and none shall be given. And my record speaks for itself.

"Love,"
Maury

Maury obviously wasn't asking for (nor taking) my advice on how to get his head straight. And yet, it's always been clear that he wanted to keep our connection going. I didn't especially feel like reading letter after letter of his violent hatreds, so I tried to slant our correspondence more toward his artwork and the family stuff he related to, like building our house.

He began sending a lot more of his artwork, too, which was sensitive. But still, in every letter Maury wrote was at least a passing mention of stabbing or killing people, and a lot of racist jokes. And in my every response, I let him know that I thought he was a few quarts low. We've stayed straight with each other right down the line.

Once after reading one of his super-angry letters, I wrote out a short fairy tale that I asked him to illustrate for me. I called it "The Convict and the Kittycat," and it must have hit him just right, because he opened up quite a bit. This was his response:

Dear Bo,
    I'm very impressed by the concise, heart-rending short story you wrote about the kitty cat. That story really "touched home. . . ." It's very prison oriented, for many prisons have cats for mascots. We had a legend here named "canteen Tom," one tough ol' perverted cat (he raped skunks—true!).
    Bo, you impressed me with your sensitivity. Never since I read Kahlil Gibran have I encountered a male who is "evolved enough" to express such sensitive feelings! I really HATE "men;" they're crude, fatuous, bellicose, vulgar—I regard men as dirty filthy brute beasts which are incapable of rational behavior.
    You, Bo, really surprise me. You're an exception to my opinion of men. You're more highly evolved; you function upon a superior level of consciousness than the majority of men do.
    Hey Bo, I felt my ego was dead—but when I got that issue of the Prison-Ashram Project newsletter and saw my envelope art on the cover ("E.T.")—gosh, what a LIFT! It copied so well it looks better than my original!
    I love you folks like you're kin of mine—and that's 'cause violent as I am, I identify with your level of consciousness. Just remember, I'm a reflection of everyone I meet. Those who come to me with sensitivity and compassion, intelligence, receive back the same from me. Those who come to me in ignorance and violence get back the same—10 times worse. Y'all take care,

Love,
Maury

Maury went on to talk about his growing friendship and respect for two women psychologists, Charlotte and Brenda. He refused to speak to any men. However, much to his dismay, Charlotte and Brenda had both resigned by the time I got his letter. He was still in touch with Brenda via mail, but now she was no more directly available to him than I was.

He also sent me a newspaper article from the *Tulsa Tribune* (June 14, 1983) that featured him and another lock-up inmate under the title "Hate-filled Convicts Become Like Animals." Maury was clearly proud that the article described him as one of the most dangerous convicts in the state. But what struck me more, was the remarkable likeness between the newspaper photo of him and the character he drew for "The Convict and The Kittycat." As we kept writing, every now and then he seemed to be softening:

Dear Bo,

Mahatma Gandhi said prison is a place for robbers, "but for me it's a temple." I admire Gandhi—he's intrepid! The authorities tried to hire an assassin to waste Gandhi in prison. Gandhi heard about it—and confronted his would-be assassin—and said, "I hear you're looking to kill me; so I delivered myself to you." And the killer turned away shamefacedly from this little 90-lb., toothless, brave little man. Gandhi's spirit gots BIG HEART.

Bo, I confess you're right about my needed being stuck on violence. I need to get my mind off this hold for awhile! Violence is becoming the total content of my thoughts! Bo, I'm really starting to "lose it." I have a permanent anxious/panicky feeling I've been experiencing lately. I used to get it about twice each year but it would leave after a couple of days. But this time it's lasted three weeks and is intensifying. It's the same kind of panic one feels after awakening in a coffin underground. I'm not exaggerating; that's how intense it is. I'm introverting more each day . . . once my introversion is complete, I shall mentally ostracize myself from this entire world and its worthless inhabitants—I shall never speak nor write to another person as long as I live. My request for correspondence is the cry of a drowning man reaching out for a little assistance—before the final descent into . . . madness.

Later,
Maury

Dear Maury,

I feel bad that you're in such low spirits. You're my friend and I love you. I just wish you could see that your own hatred-and-violence trip is killing you; it's not just being in the hole, I swear! I do believe you're going to succeed in driving yourself crazy if you keep trying so hard. Do you think it's just a coincidence that you're losing your mind, and your mind is filled with hatred? When are you going to cop to what's happening?

You've definitely succeeded in making the point that you're a big, dangerous man. So now what? You're going to be awfully embarrassed when you die and look around the astral planes and see that the size of your arms and color of your skin meant nothing at all. You say you respect Gandhi so much, but then you live exactly the opposite of everything he stood for. (By the way, his biceps were skinny and his skin was brown!)

Listen Maury, you and I have been friends for a lot of years now and you have to admit I've never tried to forcibly change you. And even now, I'm not doing that, so don't get me wrong. The only reason I'm harping on this stuff is that you're the one who keeps writing me that you're coming apart at the seams. I hurt when you hurt; that's how it is with friends. It's like I'm watching you butt your head up against the wall, and you keep crying that your head hurts. You and you alone—not the prison, not the hole, not your past—are responsible for the state of your own mind. Nobody, including me or Brenda, will be able to save your sanity if you keep up this super-macho, super-bitter routine which you've perfected. You'll just shut me and Brenda out eventually, claiming that we've become "ignorant" or something.

There's an old saying: The only way out is through. You've got so much pain to unlock and let go of; it's going to be tough and scary, but you can do it right where you are. The inner journey is more real than anything else you're experiencing, and there is relief from everything that hurts so badly.

We're praying for you, pal.

I love you,
Bo

Maury replied with some great sketches and a note saying he felt a little better, having found a new (woman) pen-pal and therefore some "escapism" from the hole. He closed with:

I'm trying to re-adjust to the conduct espoused by you and Brenda – I'm making an honest attempt. I shared your letters with Brenda; she cheers everything you say (especially where you said I was a few quarts low when it came to violence and racism). It's like listening to an echo, both of you are giving me the same advice. Between her and you, I'm succumbing to your peer pressure. Bo I know both of you love me and know what's best for me. I haven't taken advice from anyone in years. But I know you and Brenda are right. Trying to clean up my act. heh heh.

Love, "too cool fool,"
Maury

[In early April, 1985, Maury was stabbed to death by two other inmates while taking a shower. This note has been included so that we may all take Maury into our hearts and wish him well on his journey.]

Questions

1. In the case of Maury, how does Bo respond to the intense anger, bitterness, and cynicism that are evident in Maury's letters?

2. Why was the fairy tale about the "Convict and the Kittycat" that Bo asked Maury to illustrate useful in helping him get past his anger into his fear?

3. How was Brenda, the psychologist, an important bridge in Maury's journey toward peace?

4. Why was Maury finally able to trust Bo and Brenda?

5. Whatever form or expression it takes, when we use violent means to respond to violent act, what do we end up with?

The Victim's View

Whether criminal or law-abiding, we all know how it feels to be, in one way or another, both victim and offender. Whether betraying a friend's confidence or having our own heart broken, whether bearing or instigating psychological or physical assault, we each, in our own way, have experienced the two extremes. What are we inclined to want when we are the injured party—the victim? Too often it is revenge or retribution. How about when we are the perpetrator of the injury? Usually we want forgiveness, another chance.

Tom & Donny

Dear Bo,

I just re-read your newsletter for March, 1982, and once again your philosophy has touched me.

In 1968, I was beaten, tortured, and gang-raped in a county jail. This took place over a 24-hour period during which, besides the "usual" brutality of such incidents, I was also wrapped up in a sheet and set on fire. My attackers urinated on me to put it out. Although I was released two weeks later, I never really left it emotionally. Emotionally, the clock stopped for me on October 15, 1968. Few days have gone by since, that I haven't experienced at least a few moments of shame and self-disgust and the wish for death.

For the first few years, I numbed myself with marijuana. But after I stopped using drugs in '72, I slipped into a depression that lasted until 1980 when I finally began therapy. After two years of therapy, my rage is greater than ever. And now my rape may be a factor in the break-up of my 12-year marriage. A therapist has warned me that I may have become obsessed with being heard about my assault because of so long a silence.

For the two years before my rape, I had been a full-time political activist living in the barrios of San Antonio. I published and edited a tiny liberal com-

munity paper in Spanish and English. I often marched and demonstrated alone against poverty, against the Vietnam War, against discrimination and injustice of any kind. I was in jail for smashing two closed-circuit tv cameras in a restroom of a factory, to help workers publicize their grievances and win their strike. It was my first offense.

You said "our greatest acts of violence are how we constantly judge others." I understand these words but I feel so powerless to rid my heart of the desire for revenge. I know how overloaded you are with pleas of help from prisons all over the country, but in your prayers, could you please remember me? I do the same for you and all the brothers and sisters in the Prison-Ashram Project.

On my forty-sixth birthday, February 14, I began fasting from solid food. On Feb. 22nd I cloistered myself inside my leaky, uninsulated camper. I am also not speaking. I communicate only in writing. I am withdrawing from society and—if necessary—from life, unless I am blessed with justice and/or enlightenment.

God bless you for your wonderful work.

Tom

Dear Tom,

You're certainly in our prayers, and in the prayers of thousands of people who may read this. I really don't know whether anything I put into words will help you at all, but I'll try. Maybe between the lines we can communicate as if I were sitting next to you in your camper. I wish I could be.

You know that I've been involved for a long time now with people who have gone through the same sort of nightmare as you. I've never met anyone who had an easy time of it, or who looked back and said "boy, I sure am glad that happened!" So I won't try to snow you with any spiritual fairy tales. There are some terribly painful things that can happen to us in life, and you've been through one of the worst imaginable. That's the way things are.

But it's possible to come out of it with both your sanity and humanity intact, and even stronger than ever. Jesus's response to humiliation and torture has endured as an inspiration to the human spirit for thousands of years. Since you describe yourself as an activist, standing up for truth and justice, maybe now you're being given the opportunity to really be an activist, like Jesus was. Maybe this is the excruciating degree of compassion, pain, and forgiveness required to bring about truly effective social change; change which lasts.

I know it's tempting for you to say that no one could understand what you've been through. In one sense that's surely true, and it would be arrogant of me to say how I would handle your situation if it happened to me. But in another sense—a deeper one—all of us really do understand the pain, fear, loneliness, shame, and despair that you've described. It just comes in different forms, that's all.

When I was 18, I had a 100-mph head-on crash with a tractor trailer. I've gone through a lot of operations and intense pain during the past 20 years, and I can remember times when the pain just wore me down so much that I didn't know if I could keep going through it. Many times I squeaked by on the thinnest shred of faith or Grace; who knows which? I became addicted to painkillers, went through periods of denial, over-exertion, depression and oceans of self-pity. And like you, I also heard about things like meditation and yoga and the whole spiritual trip.

I noticed that when I was able to open around the pain rather than trying to push it away, every now and then I experienced the "transcendence" that all the spiritual teachers talk about. Pain still hurts like hell during those times (like the Buddha said, "Pain will always be inherently unpleasant; that's just its nature"), but you can get so big that you're able to allow it to be just what it is. It no longer takes you over so fully; it no longer plunges you into despair. And the pain brings so much wisdom, humility, patience and other good lessons, eventually we come to appreciate its divine purpose in our lives.

You can say that my pain is different from yours, and yours is different from the young mother whose child was raped and murdered, and from my Canadian friend who fell off a mountain and is permanently paralyzed, and from all the other people in the world who meet an endless variety of suffering during their lives. But pain is pain is pain, if we're willing to open up rather than shut ourselves down. If you look perhaps more openly than you have, you can find in your wife, your therapist, your neighbors and everyone else, a place which understands your suffering more than you've been willing to appreciate.

But what more can I say to you while it's hurting so much? These may sound like meaningless words as you sit in your camper wishing that half your life hadn't happened like it did. I send this letter more as a token of my love and friendship rather than an eloquent argument for or against any point of view. If you do decide to come through this instead of ending your life, just imagine the depth of compassion and understanding you can offer to others who suffer in their own forms of hell. I hope for you, me, and for the world, that you can emerge from this struggle as a true spiritual activist, with a loving heart which has been forged in the hottest fire of pain.

Love,
Bo

Dear Bo,

Just received your wonderful letter. It really has brightened my day. What you had to pass on to me is really good and clear medicine.

I have been sweating out a lot of demons in my "cloister." This is the thirteenth day in my truck and the 22ⁿᵈ of my fast. I think I will be leaving the truck and breaking my fast in a few days. For one thing, my family is taking it very hard. They think I want to die, but they are only partially right.

Anyway, I'm feeling much better and clearer, and your letter has really helped. I'll treasure the letter in my spiritual diary and I'm sure that I will often refer to it in the future whenever I'm wrestling with my demons.

I would like to rest now, so I'll close. Thank you and may the light continue shining on you.

Tom

[The late Donny, aka Robert Martin, was a published writer who experienced nearly unimaginable horrors being raped more than 50 times in a 24-hour period after being thrown in the D.C. jail due to a political protest. Some years afterward, while in federal prison, he wrote me asking for help in setting up a network of pen-pals especially for prison punks. Here is an edited version of that correspondence.]

Dear Bo,

My impression after reading your stuff was that sexuality was noticeable for its absence, and that your readers were living lives of enforced (if not voluntary) celibacy. But this is not in accord with my own experiences and extensive knowledge of prison and jail life, which is drenched with sexuality, both consensual and coerced.

Jail punks are more oppressed than any other group within the walls, living lives of abject slavery, sold and traded among the powerful, forced into prostitution, tossed about as footballs and prizes in racial and other power structures, tormented by conflicts over their sexual identity and role, isolated, humiliated, ashamed, and often suicidal. There's a crying need for someone to reach out to punks, someone who understand oppression.

I am suggesting primarily a network of pen-pals. I believe these should in the first instance be heterosexual or bisexual women, ideally young women, both because women are more likely to be able to deal with rape victims and help them to understand the nature of their oppression, and because it is vital that the punks' need for feminine contact be supported.

I'm 95 days into my solitary retreat now, with no end in sight. The period in solitary has been a real blessing so far, but signs of stress are beginning to manifest. More grist for the mindful mill.

May all be happy!
Donny the Punk/Ct.

Dear Donny,

Certainly the problems of punks are terrible, and need to be dealt with far better than anything that's currently going on. But your idea for a network of pen-pals doesn't strike me as workable.

It seems to me that this planet can hardly survive one more special interest group. A feeling of group identity may feel great and be very valuable at first, but it needs to be quickly expanded to an identity with the whole human race. Instead, what's starting to happen is that in addition to the separateness many of us unfortunately feel due to race, religion, color, or sex, we're now adding whole new labels by which we can feel disconnected from the person next door. From where I sit, humanity as a whole is not necessarily being brought closer together by this tidal wave of "you can't understand me unless you're like me" support groups.

The bottom line is, everyone suffers. Everyone truly knows loneliness, pain, humiliation and defeat. I agree with you that we need to open our eyes more to the suffering of punks, but I don't think reinforcing their identity as punks is the solution.

I really do feel your compassion and your desire to serve others. My own instincts are that it would be more useful to remind punks that their "punk-hood" is not the center of their lives. If they feel that it is, then that's the problem to work on; see what I mean? Let's keep in touch and see whether we can figure something out together.

Love,
Bo

Dear Bo,

I am sensitive to the matter of proliferating narrow-issue groups. One important distinction you should keep in mind is that most punks would give their left testicle to escape from that identity. As I envisioned it, the support would facilitate that rather than strengthen the identity. In concrete terms, everyone in his environment treats the punk as a punk. To those on the street who communicate with him, he cannot ever be open about the most important aspects of his life experiences, for fear that knowledge of his "loss of manhood" will spread in his home community. Our hypothetical pen-pal would be precisely someone with whom he can discuss everything, yet know that the person outside sees him as a person and relates to him as a person.

Bo, my writing and working on the rape question and the enslavement of punks (and gays) poses a major dilemma for my own spiritual work, though I am hardput to articulate it. It is work in the plane of duality, of concepts, and everything I do in it reinforces my own identity as a punk, since I am speaking out of experience. It would be a lot easier to just work on my own invisibility and blur my identities rather than sharpen one of them. By compassion must operate on that level, so in a sense it is the old Bodhisattva dilemma of trying to help beings while not losing track of the reality that there are no beings to help.

Perhaps one reason why I work to help other punks in transcending their punk identity, is that the destructive results of assuming that identity are all too manifest in my own life—where the identity has become so firmly attached as to be part of my own name, "Donny the Punk." Oh physician how to heal thyself?

May all be happy,
Donny the Punk

Dear Donny,

I really value your insights and I'm learning a lot from you, though I still don't agree with your proposal. In fact, the last paragraph of your letter pushed me further away from agreement than ever.

You mentioned "blurring your identities," but your spiritual work isn't a matter of "blurring" anything; if that's all it were, you could do it with booze or drugs. The spiritual path is to not cling to any identities, but let them come and go as necessary. As Ram Dass puts it, "Grab tightly, let go lightly." It sounds like you've grabbed tightly to your punk identity but forgotten how to let go at all. And this has been my concern about your proposal all along.

The other thing is, Bodhisattvas don't have an "old dilemma." Bodhisattvas are enlightened people who stick around to help others become enlightened. You and I are simply not in that league. We're not free enough to "sacrifice" our own development for the sake of others. Anything you do which hurts yourself is not going to be for the good of others. The best thing you can do for others is to get free of all your identities, confusion, and conflicts.

You said that punks need to be able to write about "the most important aspects of their life experiences," meaning their "punkhood." But that's where you and I fundamentally disagree. I don't see victimization, violence, or sexuality being "the most important aspect" of anyone's life. It may be the most painful, the most challenging, the most demanding, but not the most important. The most important aspect of any of our lives is to get free. And I hear you yearning to be free, yet then imprisoning yourself once again by signing "Donny the Punk."

I honestly think the best service you could perform for punks is to struggle free of the stranglehold this identity has on your life. Calling yourself "Donny the Punk" is like somebody calling herself "Susie the rape victim," or "Sammy who always gets mugged." If other cons cruelly call you that, that's one thing; but for you to wear it like a badge is quite a different matter.

I really feel for your suffering and send you all my blessings for your work. Your mind is sharp and your will is strong, and I have faith that someday you'll be able to cross this ocean of pain, and then be able to help many other people across as well.

Love,
Bo the human

Questions

1. How would it feel to go through what Tom and Donny experienced? Would we feel the sense of shame, rage, humiliation, and isolation that they did? Could we possibly conceive of contemplating suicide after going through such an ordeal?

2. Why is it important for Tom and Donny as well as the rest of us to "open" rather than "close- off" to our pain and work through our attachment to our identities?

3. Do we have to see ourselves in a certain way before we can become what we see?

Donna

Dear Prison-Ashram folks,

For years we have witnessed the fine work done through you all. We thank you. Now I find myself coming to you for something directly connected to my own life and family.

Our daughter, who's four, was kidnapped last summer by a two-time rapist. The police found them in 4½ hours and she was remarkably all right though much darkness went her way.

Those hours were an incredible test of our work of these past years. Between the streams of terror and panic and tears, we did all we could to surround the two of them with love, to pray, to meditate. And we found, then and afterwards, that many many people hearing of the kidnapping were stopping doing what they were doing, and doing as we were.

Police, hospital, strangers, all were surrounding us and our daughter with love. And when we got her back, she was still whole and filled with innocence, in spite of the violence and sexuality she was subjected to. She had spent most of the time talking to him, of right and wrong, of her understandings of the order around her. "I loved him a little and hated him a little" was one of the first things she told us.

Then came months of assimilating and sorting the great pain. And all that still continues, though quieter now. And during that time, the legal issues were being drawn into it. We could not find any peace in the "Catch-22"-ness of it all: Having our 4-year-old testify and be torn apart by defense lawyers; dropping the case, which was threatened if she didn't testify; sending this man back to jail which had not done him any good before, etc., etc. We were all victims.

Finally, we fasted and prayed for three days and came to a peaceful relationship to it all with this understanding. The proper responsibility in the guilt was in his hands and demanded a public confession. He did plead guilty and it was settled out of court. He was sentenced on the violated probation and on the new sentences. He stood up in court and said, facing my husband, that though he has no memory of the incident (supposedly he has blocked out the whole thing) he was sorry for all the pain he caused to our family.

So now, the children ask what he does in prison, how long he'll be there, how old they'll be when he gets out, and on and on. We wonder if our relationship to him is done. Do we have any more responsibility now than to hold him in our hearts and prayers, and do our own work to come to a full forgiveness? I still wonder if I should personally go to him or write him, to tell him all the specifics of what went on so he can come to some peace with what he did instead of spending all those years in jail for an offense he has no memory of.

All I've come up with so far is to pass his name on to you. From what I understand, he has a very mild and inward nature unless he's drinking. Maybe meditation would be a door for him. Would you send him whatever you have, and just know that he's there in case you go to his prison?

Thank you from the bottom of our hearts for all the fine work you've been doing.

In Love,
Donna/New Mexico

Dear Donna,

Sita and I thank you deeply for sharing your ordeal with us. Your letter is awe-inspiring for the compassion and consciousness you've brought to such a nightmarish experience.

I'm sure your process of "assimilating and sorting the great pain" will go on for awhile, but it sounds like your faith and vision are remarkably unclouded. It's through such pain that many of us discover what the spiritual life is really all about. The opening, deepening, pain, and wisdom all go hand in hand. Sometimes God's blessings are excruciating, but blessings all the same. It seems that you and your whole family have been given one of those.

You asked for my advice about your relationship to Oscar. I can't think of any "shoulds" or "shouldn'ts" that wouldn't sound stupid after all you've been through. Oscar has already been greatly blessed just by the fact of you being his victims. Your forgiveness and concern are profound contributions to his spiritual journey, like Jesus forgiving those who nailed Him to the cross.

My only advice is to try to be as self-honest as possible, and make sure that whatever you do is what you're able to do from the heart—not what your mind thinks you should do in order to be "good." If you're ever able to truly open to Oscar and offer him your kinship, I think that act could do more for world peace than a hundred summit conferences, because this is really the nitty-gritty of bringing God-consciousness into our worldly lives.

Our love to you all,
Bo

Questions

1. What kind of person is Donna? How is she different from many of her contemporaries?

2. How did her influence with her daughter possibly save her daughter's life?

3. What is the significance of her daughter telling her parents when she was brought home after her ordeal, "I loved him a little and hated him a little"?

4. Does forgiveness automatically exclude anger? Is there room for grief in a compassionate heart? Is forgiveness simply a decision or a process one works through and toward?

Confusing Reflections

Prison and life in general, can be very confusing. Think about the confused people you have met, including your own confused times as well. Like Gloria, at certain times in our lives, we want to "change our ways," but find that too often, like well-worn New Year's resolutions, we return to old, destructive habits. And like "A", we struggle with feeling alone and wanting to know who we are and where we belong both in and out of prison. Then there is the deeper, more severe confusion like that of Mary Jo where the pain that cannot be named is acted upon in desperate ways that bring about even more suffering.

Gloria

Bo,

I really understand what you're always saying about being simple and open, not playing games with people, and I know that's the right way to live. My problem is, I've never done anything else but play games and manipulate people. How can someone like me possibly change, when the change you're talking about is like my whole personality? Where do I start?

I hate to sound pessimistic, but at this point in my life I don't see how I can turn it all around. Conning and hustling and even lying, are lifelong habits that just keep coming up without me even trying.

Sincerely,
Gloria/N.C.

Dear Gloria,

I hear you; I really do. The thing is, first of all, who is it who wrote me such a beautiful, open letter and signed it "sincerely?" Don't overlook what's right in front of your nose: You are a good person who really wants to change in a big way. So, you're already off to a good start.

The second thing is, the ONLY way any of us ever change our old behavior patterns, is one moment at a time. When you think of changing all the millions of tiny ways you lie and hustle, you get overwhelmed and feel like you'll never make it. But the true spiritual warrior (which you really are, you know) doesn't get sucked in by that kind of future-tripping. The only lie you need to stop telling is the one that starts forming in your throat right now. The only scam you need to let go of is the one your mind is beginning to think about.

Do you see what I mean? Thinking of how big the task is, is just another cruel mind-game, just another hype to keep you from taking control of your life. Try to realize that you're at least as good in fooling yourself as you are at fooling others; so be on guard, and don't let your mind get ahead of you. Be suspicious of despair and pessimism. Find various ways to remind yourself (meditation, keeping a diary, using a mantra, etc.) of what you're trying to do, and of the fact that the real work is just one moment at a time. If we had to make huge changes up front, none of us would ever see the Light. Big change is just a bunch of little ones.

Much love and encouragement,
Bo

Question

1. Can you put yourself in the place of Gloria? At one time or another do we all play games and con or manipulate others? When we want to change our lives, do we want an easy solution or insight when it takes the commitment and perseverance of starting anew each day with the changes we want to make?

"A"

Dear Bo,

Thank you so much for coming and sharing your message with us here! I do appreciate your embrace and warmth toward me after your talk. I dig what you said about feeling my sadness to its fullest and using it to gain more empathy and compassion. I do care about others and try to spend time helping others even in here.

But one of my deepest sorrows is my aloneness. I am so jealous of the deep relationship that you and Sita have! I've spent my life in the can—never had a real love relationship. I am poignantly aware that I am missing something.

The Tao speaks of a deep need to be united with your spiritually complementary partner. Hindus too. Is it possible that I can ever feel complete while so utterly alone? Am I selfish to want this? Do I just desire this, or is it a need?

Thanks for all your love!,
A

Dear A,

I appreciate how honest you were in the workshop. You helped everyone there to open up. Thank you.

A lot of people on the streets complain that their romantic relationship is the biggest obstacle to their enlightenment. They say "if only I were single, *then* I could really do spiritual practice." I even know ex-cons who yearn for the simplicity of prison life, complaining that with family, etc., they have no time for meditation.

If we're looking for ways to feel alienated, lonely, and worried, we'll find them. Sita and I are in a relationship, so that's our circumstance to work with. You find yourself *not* in a romantic relationship, so that's your circumstance. We all have the same choice. To use all our circumstances toward spiritual goals. There are always hard parts of that choice.

And being alone is extremely different from being lonely. Since you quoted from the Tao, I should mention that Lao Tzu and other Taoist Masters lived in extreme solitude most of their lives—a lot longer than you've been in prison. They chose to be alone.

Being honest with your experience of sadness is important, but justifying the sadness with a philosophy about "complementary partners" is a whole other thing.

I am sympathetic, you know that. But the whole universe exists right where you are. Bear in mind as you move through your experiences of sadness, regret, longing, etc., that one day you will feel whole and complete, right where you are.

If you can find your completeness in prison, then it will follow you to the street, into a relationship or anywhere else you ever find yourself. If you don't find your completeness where you are, then it won't be "waiting" for you anywhere else. Check out the divorce rate!

If you can find a way to accept your present "assignment" with all your energy, you'll be living as fulfilling a life as Sita & me. Really. We believe in you and love you very much. You have a big heart and a good mind.

Your friend,
Bo

Question

1. When responding to "A", what does Bo mean concerning the difference between "being lonely and being alone"? What are some of the possible benefits of learning to be alone with ourselves?

Mary-Jo

To Bo Lozoff:

My name is Mary-Jo. I spoke to you when you came to Prison for Women. I am 18 years of age. I enjoyed the peaceful feeling after I meditate; but someone told me all this stuff about spirits drowning my spirit, my spirit could get lines crossed and I could go into a coma for the rest of my life. Is this true?

Let me tell you about myself first before you answer. Age-wise I am 18, but mentally I am 13-14 years of age. I am very naive about a lot of things.

I was taken out of my natural home when I was three. I was moved from foster home to foster home until I was 7. Between the ages of 7-12 I can't remember. Most of my memory has returned after a year of who I was. When I was charged the cops tole me something that was very upsetting which I was in shock for quite awhile. But I lived a year in total darkness of who I was, why I was in jail, etc.

I hope I am not boring you but I felt I should tell someone what is going on in my head because the shrink or psychologist doesn't understand the real me. They want a false person. I try to act normal for me but then I get dirty looks or sworn at. They want a more mature person with no problems at all.

I can hold everything in me until I finally explode. What I mean is either I hurt myself or set a fire. When I told the shrink all he asked was "when were all the other explosions?" So I told him and he asked if I was ever on medication for my problem. I say no and he puts me on nerve medication.

You only talk to shrink for fifteen minutes, then he kicks you out.

I hope you understand what I am saying, if you don't please ask. I have to close now. So bye for now.

Sincerely,
Mary-Jo/Canada

P.S. I need an understanding friend.

Dear Mary-Jo,

I'm already your friend, so you don't even need to ask. Please feel free to write me anytime. I do remember you; you're the beautiful young Native-American girl who talked to me during the break about the fires you set while you were babysitting.*

It's good that you enjoyed meditation, and don't worry even slightly about crossing lines or going into a coma or being influenced by other spirits or anything like that. Meditation gives you more control, not less. It's simply a process of gradually quieting your mind, and it's very safe and has been around for thousands of years. If anything frightening ever happens while you meditate just write me about it and we'll discuss it.

You have to remember that it's fear itself that is the problem, not fear of this or fear of that. Fear is a liar. When it tells you to be scared of something, don't get into the "something," whatever it is; but instead feel the feeling of fear itself—the ugly, shrewd feeling—and don't let it take control of you. Let is pass through your body and mind like a sinister stormcloud floats through the peaceful blue sky.

Try this breathing practice when you feel fear: With your eyes closed, feel the breath come into you and bring calmness and strength in with it. Then hold your breath and let it "soak up" all the fear, worry, tension, and whatever else you want to get rid of, and then blow that out with the out-breath. Try this for awhile every day.

It seems like some things have happened to you in the past that have hurt, shocked, and frightened you very deeply. Your response to it—a very natural one—has been to block it all out of your mind. When that hasn't worked, maybe you've tried to *burn* it away. You know, fire is the great "purifier" of the universe.

I think your gut instincts have been right on, Mary-Jo, I really do. But you've been using the wrong kind of fire, and you've burned down the wrong things. The fire you're aching for is actually a very *gentle* flame—the eternal flame of your own beautiful spirit, your own heart. And what you need to burn in that fire is not buildings, or children, but rather the confusion and pain which are buried in the past. You need to burn your pain into wisdom, the impure into the pure. And you can do it now in a new way.

Try this form of meditation for awhile. Sit straight and still, eyes closed, and focus all your attention on the center of your chest, where you can imagine your spiritual heart is. Picture a small, pink flame there, flickering steadily. Imagine each breath going in right to that spot, feeding the flame. In and out, in and out, right there at the heart-space. As any scary or painful memories come up, breathe them right into that spot and watch them burn up in the flame, making the fire slightly brighter. Anything that makes you feel bad, just offer into the fire and watch it become powerless to control you.

The fires you start with matches can't burn away what you've wanted. But try this new way for awhile every day and night. The more we open our hearts to ourselves, the more we can open them to each other. The more we open our hearts, the easier it is to look at our fear and pain, and then to gradually let them burn away until we're free.

Sita and I both send our love to you. Please feel free to write us anytime, we're your family if you want us to be.

Love,
Bo

*Mary-Jo is in prison for several counts of murder by arson.

Question

1. Why did Bo use the image of "fire and flame" with Mary Jo? Think about the difference between fire being an agent for destruction and being an agent for purification and transformation.

To Help or Not to Help

For better or worse, the fates of the keepers and the kept are intertwined. Most prison workers enjoy and are encouraged to see inmates succeed and do something positive with their lives. Yet, the down-side can be burn-out as workers face unresponsive inmates and staff and scarce resources. In addition, persons from outside prison who try to help prisoners also face special challenges—how to meaningfully and effectively relate to inmates and make the most of the resources they have available.

Janet

Dear Bo,

I work in a juvenile facility here in Toronto. It's extremely depressing, and I've found myself close to quitting more than once. Unlike what you probably find in the adult prisons you visit, these young people don't seem open to positive change. Ideas like meditation and yoga—except among a very few individuals—would seem to be out of the question; and yet they need it so badly!

What do you say to someone who needs to listen, but won't? How do you reach someone who's bent on destroying his whole life? Or do you just let them do it, and then work with them ten years and ten miles down the road, in the adult institution?

Most of the staff here are really good people, and would love to find a program which would create more effective change. They care a lot, but can't seem to find the right key. Do you have one handy?

Sincerely,
Janet/Canada

Dear Janet,

The key to working with juveniles is right under our noses; it's so simple that we keep looking too far for new programs and philosophies. But the key won't be found in any program; it's found in the example we set.

Whether juveniles like to admit it or not, they're extremely impressionable to role models of the adults around them. That's how many of them got into trouble in the first place. In an adult prison, the guards aren't seen as role models. But in a juvie facility, the inmates are constantly—even subconsciously—checking out you and the other staff members to gain more understanding of their options; the range of possibilities for what kind of adults they might become.

I did a workshop at your institution a few years ago. I was invited to speak to the staff (I guess it was before you started working there). I looked around the room and saw a group of very dedicated, very caring people (as you said) but they were also chain-smoking, nail-biting, coffee-guzzling, harried, and disorganized. No matter how loving their intentions, what young offender is going to be impressed with that example of adulthood?

I really don't mean to be coming down hard on you or your colleagues, because believe me, I admire all of you tremendously. But the age is past when we can separate our own well-being from the work that we do; we know too much to be that way anymore.

The frenzied social worker who's always trying to catch up to yesterday and subsists on baloney sandwiches stuffed down in the hallways is old hat. We know now that what people really get from us is more a measure of who we are than what we say or the things we give them.

In a juvenile facility, a staff person who's calm and strong and happy is worth is or her weight in gold. People who are living examples of truthfulness, good humor, patience, and courage are going to change more lives—even if they're employed as janitors—than the counselors who can't get their own lives in order. I can't possibly stress this enough.

So, I do agree with you about the difficulties of working in a juvie prison, but at the same time I think there's not only a key, but a very exciting one at that. Just by doing your own work on yourself; by continually striving to be a shining, happy example of whatever you believe in, you will become the most powerful program the facility could ever offer.

Not all kids are ready for change. But a large proportion of them are; and you'll begin to attract them like moths to a flame; as your own light shines brighter and brighter. Much love to you and blessings for your inspired work with these children of God.

Love,
Bo

Questions

1. Imagine working in the juvenile facility where Janet works. What does it feel like? What kind of impact does the environment have on your attitude?

2. Is it, as Bo suggests, that juveniles are more affected by "what we do than what we say"? Is this also true of parent/child relationships?

3. If we want to help others change, who is only person upon whom we can really work?

"F"

Dear Bo and Sita,

Bo, I work in a Texas prison mailroom, so I really sympathize with the problem you're having getting *Lineage and Other Stories* to TDC inmates. When I was asked to read the books for unit approval, I recognized them for the beautiful spiritual tools they are, and approved them both. However, another unit denied them and when one unit denies a publication, we all have to unless otherwise directed. So that's how it happened . . . they ALMOST made it.

There are other employees who feel as I do, that there is nothing wrong with the content. There are a lot of good people too, who really care about the inmates. And you know we have to battle some pretty bad stuff Bo, like the prison gangs, drugs, hits, rapes . . . sometimes it's just awful what the inmates do to each other. But those of us that really care are there every day trying to make it better.

I've been in metaphysics about 25 years now. When I went to work for TDC I got criticized a lot by others. "How can you do it?" they would ask, insinuating that I had sold out spiritually. Little do they know I was very specifically guided there. That's where the "real" BOSS wants me. Learning and teaching and carrying my torch of love inside with me.

Knowing you and others like you reminds me we are not in this dimension alone although it can feel that way sometimes.

Take care,
F

PS: My grandson, Jamie, was born with open-cell spina bifida. The rocking-chair horse he is enjoying so much was done by an inmate, M, at the unit where I work. He was so excited to do this for Jamie, and when I brought him a print of a picture, tears came to his eyes. The craft boss tole me later that's all M talked about. Nobody ever did that for him before—bring him a picture of something he had made.

Some of our artistic inmates delight in drawing pictures for Jamie of Mickey Mouse, Donald Duck, and dogs, dogs, dogs. Jamie loves dogs. I just wish sometimes that people knew that as bad as prisons are—there's a lot of good stuff going on too.

Questions

1. Although "F" worked in the mail room in a Texas prison and was not a psychologist, counselor, or caseworker, did she have a positive, even therapeutic effect on the prisoners with whom she came in contact? How did she do it?

2.   Why did the inmate who made the rocking horse for "F"'s grandson react the way he did when "F" gave him a photograph of her grandson riding the rocking horse?

3.   How can each of us, wherever we find ourselves, be more like "F," the mail room worker?

Alan

Dear Bo,

I am a member of a Christian community. Since last spring, a co-worker and I have been working with a group of inmates at Auburn Prison. We have discovered that working as white do-gooders with a bunch of ghetto blacks is tough. Our problem right now is what to do to really help them, so we are going back to square one and re-evaluating our program with our admission that we know nothing and need help. Thus this letter.

Our first step has been to link up every inmate with a member of the Christian community on a correspondence basis. Now we have more people with a stake in our program, so it doesn't just rest on the shoulders of the two of us. Please send us any information and advice. We want both to help them on a spiritual level and work on a practical level to aid in their ability to operate in the world, etc.

Many thanks for your fine work; am looking forward to hearing from you.

Yours in Christ,
Alan/N.Y.

Dear Alan,

A couple of ideas right off the bat:

1) Come to a clearer idea of what you can best offer. The possibilities for helping prisoners are almost unlimited, but no one person or even a community can bite off the whole range. The pen-pal connection is a good idea. You also mention spiritual stuff—what form? Classes inside? Other speakers and teachers? You could organize a fellowship group among the cons themselves; you could hook up with other spiritual groups around Auburn to sponsor classes besides your own for non-Christians; etc.

The first thing you may want to do is to find out what all the community resources already are, so you can understand the bigger picture of how you may best fit in. You can ask the inmates to come up with a list of how you may best fit in. You can ask the inmates to come up with a list of ideas for needed community support, and then see whether you're able to help fill any of them. In the course of doing your homework, the answers you're looking for may start popping out from every direction. You just have to scan the situation and decide to do a few things really well, rather than a lot of things half-ass.

2) About being white do-gooders among ghetto blacks—I hear where you're coming from, but you have to expand your vision if you want to be of any real use. Yes, you're white do-gooders on one level, but on another level you're disciples of the Christ—way beyond petty details like skin color or age.

Your passion to help others is the most ancient, universal will-to-do-good that exists. If you were green or yellow, and lived in 400 BC on another planet, it would feel the same. The fact that you're white right now and the cons are mostly black is just the least detail. Think big. Be big. Otherwise, you'll just keep getting caught where some of the inmates are stuck, and then you'll all be jiving each other instead of journeying down the path.

I guess that's the bottom line that I want to emphasize to you: You, ultimately, have to decide what it is you're able to do. Don't fall into the classic "naive liberal" trap of being so intimidated by race and personal history, that you just become a doormat for the people you wish to help. You'll burn out that way, and you won't really help anyone in the long run. You have to do whatever you do with joy and interest, and you can't let the cons define who they want you to be to them. You have to figure out who you are, and then share yourself with love.

Love,
Bo

Question

1. What do think about Bo's advice to Alan regarding helping inmates, particularly concerning his being white and the majority of them being black?

2. Have you ever attended with a group to help the elderly at a nursing home or other environment where you felt somewhat out-of-place and didn't know exactly what to do? Is important when we find ourselves in such situations to keep an open and willing heart and do whatever we can, no matter how small, to help?

Hope Remains

Mental and emotional prisons can be more confining and devastating than prisons made of concrete and steel. When even a small amount of hope remains, the unlikely becomes possible. Sometimes the long-shot comes in and we are always amazed when it does. Hope helps us to try again, even when the odds are so long, we almost can't see them.

Larry and Yusufu

Dear Bo,

My name is Larry, and I have been pen-pals with Yusufu for six years. His was the third name I got from you, the first two did not respond to my letters. Yusufu did answer, and has continued to for six years. We write about once a month, sometimes more, sometimes less. He has been an inspiration to me on many occasions. To be in jail and to work on your consciousness and spiritual development is to plunge into a cleansing fire daily. His commitment hasn't wavered as far as I've ever seen. Getting a letter from him usually makes my day.

Last year I visited him for the first time. The person who I met face-to-face was authentic and true to the person in his letters. Truthfully, I was surprised. Surprised at his willingness to expose himself in front of other prisoners, and that there wasn't a different person in person than in correspondence.

I'm not sure what I want to tell you. My life is richer for having known Yusufu. He has allowed me to peek into a world hidden away from my normal surroundings. His example astonished me, because I doubt I'd be so strong or open in his situation—and if he can do it there—I can do it here.

He has given me the honor of touching his life. He has shown me how one can rise above the most corrupting influences, and learn to love in an unloving place. I think the only real teaching one can do is by example, and so, you have allowed me to hook up not with just another spiritual seeker (and certainly not a Sunday-morning seeker), but with a spiritual teacher. I thank and honor you for your work.

Larry/California

Dear Bo and Sita,

A month or so ago, I suggested to a close friend of mine, Larry, that we both write you a thank-you letter for bringing us together about six or seven years ago. We have continually written one another throughout this time, and we've grown very, very close. We write about once or twice a month, covering a variety of topics, the most important of which has been our spiritual journeys.

It has not been easy for me—I'm in my tenth year and I've had many personal tragedies to affect me—but the worst parts of my life are only minor by comparison to my righteous spiritual friendship with Larry.

In 1982, he stopped in here for a surprise visit. He lives in California, the prison I live in is in southern Illinois. We had exchanged pictures and talked deeply about ourselves, but nothing was more beautiful than our first meeting in the flesh in the visiting room. He is white and I am black, so you can imagine how we must have looked in the visiting room with other visi-

tors, who were all white. The Larry I had come to know in my letters was the very same Larry I met then; we had a very beautiful and delightful time.

Larry has really sharpened my spiritual practice, and has shown me most accurately that it's not words that counts so much as deeds. Many guys are always looking for someone to write, but it's always a female, not a male. Admittedly, I'd like to be able to write a female too, but as Larry has shown me over the years, I can grow to/with a male just as I can with a female.

It has been a real loving, caring, sharing and growing experience, and I am certain that it will last a lifetime (and beyond). And it is all due to your willingness to step outside societal prejudice and connect the seekers of this world, inside and out. I thank you and the ashram project very deeply for your work and bringing Larry into my life. The gifts of peace, happiness, and most of all, love, be with you all, always.

Yusufu

Question

1. How does the example of "Larry and Yusufu" demonstrate the potential for letter writing in terms of one finding peace and personal growth through a relationship with another?

"M"

Dear Bo & Sita,

You haven't heard from me since 1977, when I was at the Diagnostic Center. At that time another convict turned me on to a well-worn copy of Inside Out. [Inside Out *is now called* We're All Doing Time.] *Using some of the tapes you sent, we started our own meditation class. Although it was only seven inmates, we had some powerful, wonderful experiences. Within a year we all transferred to different locations and the class was no more, but it was a huge success while it lasted.*

I feel my spirit grow and I learned so much from you & Sita. But after being released somehow I began to backslide. And now here I am doing time again.

I thought about you two many times over the years. And you have had a profound effect on my life. In your eyes what you do may not seem so significant, but please believe me, you are shaking people's lives to the very core. I consider meeting you the most important event in my life. Without you I would still be lost in the grid.

I had lost hope of finding you again, when out of the blue I stumbled across a copy of We're All Doing Time. *And after all the nickel-dime novels—what a breath of fresh air! Thank you so much for doing what you do. You've given so many of us that little push we need to get us on the right path.*

Bo & Sita, before I close I would like to relate a little story to you about how powerful your work really is. It was Christmas 1977 and men were feeling low at the institution as is true at most prisons near Christmas. I'd been abandoned and didn't receive much mail—so when my name was called at mail call there was a little stir among the inmates. (The same inmates usually got mail over & over.) You and Sita had sent me a Christmas card—the only one I received that year. I was awed that someone I barely knew would take the time to send a card. I was yelling the news to a friend several cells down and my next door neighbor overheard. Now my neighbor was a very notorious individual. 300 pounds of pure hate. He would make Freddy Kruger seem like John Boy Walton! Anyway, he overheard about the card and slyly began questioning me. He's like—"Hey man let me look at the card—I just want to see if I know them." I pass the card over—he studies it for a long time and says something about you're just a couple of weirdos. I told him about your books and tapes but he made it very clear he wasn't interested. He was not the kind of guy you push so I just let it go. News was all over the cell block about the card and it was passed around. Next day my book and tapes disappear while I'm on the yard. It was the first time in my life that it actually felt good to have something taken from me. A week later the book and tapes mysteriously reappeared on my bed. No one ever copped out to taking them, but sometimes late at night I could hear a very low chanting noise coming from Freddy Kruger's cell. And did that dude ever change! He actually started being nice to people. He eventually dropped his tough guy image and within the next year became more and more like a giant 300 pound lamb. What a drastic change. And it all began with a Christmas wish and a little card from Bo & Sita!

I know firsthand the power of your lessons and your advice. And after 20 years you're still at it. Thank God for brothers and sisters like Bo & Sita. It's great to see some of your material again. We're All Doing Time *is Right On!*

Gotta go for now. Please take care.

Love Always,
M (Georgia)

Questions

1. The small gesture of sending a Christmas card with a lot of love and care to an inmate who feels forgotten can have unforseen consequences. How did the card and those who sent it become peacemaking catalysts for the personal transformation of an aggressive 300-pound inmate?

2. A brief note or phone call to an elderly person or shut-in seems a minor thing. Can such an act when done with a loving and caring attitude, result in bringing great joy and hope to the one who receives it? Mother Teresa once talked of doing "small things with great love." Can each of us participate in such a process?

Come, come, whoever you are,
wanderer, worshiper, lover of leaving;
Come, ours is not a caravan of despair.
Though you've broken your vow a thousand times,
Come, come again.

– Rumi

All sorrows can be borne if you put them into a story . . .
— Isak Dinesen

Distrust all men in whom the impulse to punish is powerful.
— Friedrich Nietzsche

Where there is life, there is hope.
— Latin proverb

Chapter 7
Prison Stories

This chapter is based upon the writings of Jarvis Masters, who currently resides on Death Row at San Quentin State Prison.[1] Born in 1962, Jarvis was separated from his siblings and raised in foster care because his mother was addicted to drugs and his father had abandoned the family. For awhile Jarvis was content, but when the couple he was staying with became too old to care for him, his life took on a more destructive pattern. From nine or 10 years of age throughout his teen years, Jarvis was often in trouble and was a ward of the state. He was known as a young person who had a good sense of humor and a great deal of potential, but who continued in a downward spiral. When he was 17, he was released from the California Youth Authority and while he did not shoot anyone, he proceeded to hold up a string of stores and restaurants. Eventually he was caught and sent to San Quentin. Jarvis was 19 when he arrived at San Quentin. He joined a gang as many inmates do. In the course of events that followed, a correctional officer was killed. Jarvis was one of three inmates who were tried for the murder of the correctional officer. An older inmate ordered the killing, another inmate actually stabbed the officer, and Jarvis was accused of sharpening the metal that was used to stab the officer. For a variety of reasons, including Jarvis's violent past, he was the only one of the three given the death sentence. Jarvis had been on death row since 1990. Facing the possibility of death in such a situation tends to either harden one's heart or soften it; close one off or open one up. Since 1990, Jarvis has been through many changes. He has taken responsibility for the choices he has made. He has evolved through studying the practice of Buddhism to the point of dedicating himself to the practice of compassion and nonviolence to however long he has left. As he continues the appeals process through state and federal courts, Jarvis continues to write about the challenges and opportunities to be a peacemaker in the midst of a violent world. Each of the following excerpts are followed by questions for reflection and discussion.

Scars

I remember the first time I really noticed the scars on the bodies of my fellow prisoners. I was outside on a maximum-custody exercise yard. I stood along the fence, praising the air the yard gave my lungs that my prison cell didn't. I wasn't in a rush to pick up a basketball or do anything. I just stood in my own silence.

I looked at the other prisoners, playing basketball or handball, showering, talking to one another. I saw the inmates I felt closest to, John, Pete, and David, lifting weights. I noticed the amazing similarity of the whiplike scars on their bare skin, shining with sweat from pumping iron in the hot sun.

A deep sadness came over me as I watched these powerful men lift hundreds of pounds of weights over their heads. I looked around the yard and made the gruesome discovery that everyone else had the same deep gashes – behind their legs, on their backs, all over their ribs – evidence of the violence in our lives.

Here were America's lost children – surviving in rage and in refuge from society. I was certain that many of their crimes could be traced to the horrible violence done to them as children.

The histories of all of us in San Quentin were too similar – it was as if we had the same parents. Though I was a trusted comrade of most of these inmates, and to a few of them I was their only family, normally I wouldn't dare intrude on their private pain. Even so, I made up my mind that I would bring John, Pete, and David together to talk about their scars. These men had probably never spoken openly of their terrible childhood experiences. I doubted that any of them would ever have used the word "abuse." They looked hardened to the core, standing around the weight-lifting bench, proud of their bodies and the images they projected.

It occurred to me, as I approached them, that such a posture of pride symbolized the battles they had "made their bones" with. This was prison talk that "proved their manhood." At one time I had been hardened as well and had made my own denials. The difficulty I would have in speaking with them would be interpreting the prison language we all used when talking about our pasts. Shucking and jiving was the way we covered up sensitive matters.

John was a 28-year-old bulky man serving 25 to life for murder. I had met him when we were both in youth homes in southern California. We were only 11 years old. Throughout the years, we traveled together through the juvenile system until the penitentiary became our final stop.

When I asked him about the scars on his face he said, "They came from kickin' ass and, in the process, getting my ass kicked, which was rare."

John explained that his father had loved him enough to teach him how to fight when he was only five years old. He learned from the beatings he got. In a sense, he said, he grew up with a loving fear of his father. He pointed to a nasty scar on his upper shoulder. Laughing, he told us that his father had hit him with a steel rod when John tried to protect his mother from being beaten.

Most of us had seen this scar but had never had the nerve to ask about it. As we stared at it, John seemed ashamed. Avoiding our eyes, he mumbled a few words before showing us his many other scars. He could remember every detail surrounding the violent events that had produced them. I realized that these experiences haunted him. Yet as he went on talking, he became increasingly rational. He had spent more than one-half of his life in one institutional setting or another, and as a result he projected a very cold and fearsome, almost boastful smile. He wanted nothing of what he shared with us to be interpreted, even remotely, as child abuse.

This was especially apparent when he showed us a gash on his back that was partially hidden by a dragon tattoo. It was a hideous scar – something I would have imagined finding on a slave who had been whipped. John motioned me closer and said, "Rub your finger down the dragon's spine." I felt what seemed like thick, tight string that moved like a worm beneath his skin.

"Damn, John, what in the hell happened to you?" I asked.

There was something in the way I questioned him that made John laugh, and the others joined in. He explained that when he was nine his father chased him with a cord. John ran under a bed, grabbed the springs, and held on as his father pulled him by the legs, striking his back repeatedly with the cord until he fell unconscious. He woke up later with a deep flesh wound. John, smiling coldly, joked that that was the last time he ever ran from his father.

David and Pete recounted similar childhood experiences. Their stories said much about how all of us had come to be in one of the worst prisons in the country. Most prisoners who were abused as children were taken from their natural parents at a very early age and placed in foster homes, youth homes, or juvenile halls for protection, where they acquired even more scars. Later in their lives prisons provided the same kind of painful refuge. It is terrifying to realize that a large percentage of prisoners will eventually reenter society, father children, and perpetuate what happened to them.

Throughout my many years of institutionalization, I, like so many of these men, unconsciously took refuge behind prison walls. Not until I read a series of books for adults who had been abused as children did I become committed to the process of examining my own childhood. I began to unravel the reasons I had always just expected to go from one youth institution to the next. I never really tried to stay out of these places, and neither did my friends.

That day I spoke openly to my friends about my physical and mental abuse as a child. I told them that I had been neglected and then abandoned by my parents, heroin addicts, when I was very young. I was beaten and whipped by my stepfather. My mother left me and my sisters alone for days with our newborn twin brother and sister when I was only four years old. The baby boy died of crib death, and I always believed it was my fault, because I had been made responsible for him. I spoke to them of the pain I had carried through more than a dozen institutions, pain I could never face. And I explained how all of these events ultimately trapped me in a pattern of lashing out against everything.

But these men could not think of their own experiences as abuse. What I had told them seemed to sadden them, perhaps because I had embraced a hidden truth that they could not. They avoided making the connection between my experiences and theirs. It was as if they felt I had suffered more than they. That wasn't true. What they heard was their own unspoken words.

Eventually, we all fell silent around the weight-lifting bench, staring across the yard at the other men exercising.

John and I spoke again privately later. "You know something?" he said. "The day I got used to getting beaten by my father and by the counselors in all those group homes was the day I knew nothing would ever hurt me again. Everything I thought could hurt me I saw as a game. I had nothing to lose and just about everything to gain. A prison cell will always be here for me."

John was speaking for most of the men I had met in prison. Secretly, we like it here. This place welcomes a man who is full of rage and violence. He is not abnormal here, not different. Prison life is an extension of his inner life.

Finally, I confided to John that I wished I had been with my mother when she died.

"Hey, didn't you say she neglected you?" he asked.

John was right, she had neglected me, but am I to neglect myself as well by denying that I wished I'd been with her when she died, that I still love her?

Questions

1. Although most of us don't bear the physical scars that Jarvis and his friends carry with them, many of us do have as a remnant of our childhood or past relationship, some degree of emotional and mental scarring. How do such scars affect us? Can they place us in an "inner" prison?

2. Why do you think it seemed so important to some of the men that Jarvis talked with that they interpreted the violence they suffered from their parents as love? What is the role of humor in dealing with such abuse?

3. Can institutions of corrections also produce "scars" on those persons who are incarcerated? (On those who work there?) Can the same be said of institutions of education? Just as various social institutions can be catalysts for hope and positive change, they can also become instruments for despair, hopelessness, and cynicism.

For a Long Time

For a long time I had been my own stranger, but everything I went through in learning how to accept myself brought me to the doorsteps of dharma, the Buddhist path.

During my death penalty trial, Melody, a private investigator working on my case, sent me books on how to meditate, how to deal with pain and suffering, how to keep my mind at rest. She had broken her ankle and was trying to keep still. She and I were both trying this meditation gig, and like me, she was confronting a lot of things in her past. She was also writing and encouraged me to do so as well.

I began to get up early to try to calm my mind so I wouldn't panic. It was as if my whole life was being displayed on a screen during the death penalty case. Things I had never realized about myself and my life were introduced to me and the jury at the same time. Questions I'd never asked my mother – like how long she'd been abused, on the street, an addict – were being asked now. Through meditation I learned to slow down and take a few deep breaths, to take everything in, not to run from the pain, but to sit with it, confront it, give it the companion it had never had. I became committed to my meditation practice.

While I was in the holding booth during the jury's deliberation on whether I should get life without parole or the death penalty, I started leafing through a Buddhist journal Melody had left there. In it was an article called "Life in Relation to Death" by a Tibetan Buddhist lama, Chagdud Tulku Rinpoche. I thought, "Wow! This is right up my alley!"

I sent a letter to the address in the journal and got a reply from a woman named Lisa, one of Rinpoche's close students, with a copy of his booklet, *Life in Relation to Death*. At the time, I'd gotten into some kind of trouble and was in isolated confinement, stripped down to a pair of shorts and a T-shirt, with only two blankets. In her letter, Lisa asked if I needed help. I always needed help, I still need help, and because of the help she offered, we began corresponding. Then she began to visit me and eventually brought Rinpoche to San Quentin.

When I first saw Rinpoche through the glass in the small visiting room booth, I thought, "Oh, shit, I'm in trouble now. I'm messing around with a real lama. He's from Tibet. Check him out. I bet everything he's got on is blessed."

I figured there were two ways I could introduce myself. I could greet him in an ordinary way, or I could bow. I bowed. Then he bowed. Why'd I think he wouldn't? He's been bowing all his life.

I thought, "I've been reading about lamas for the last three years and now I have a real one in front of me." I knew that all I could do was tell him exactly what I think. If I lied or shied away from him, he'd know it.

I fell in love with him for the same reasons everybody else does. His life history was my key. He had been a rebellious kid. He wasn't born with a silver spoon. He was a feisty guy who would discipline me when I needed it. He knew what he was talking about, and would say it in a way that I'd get it. He had a certain shrewdness. Compassionate ferociousness. He was a lama who ate beef jerky, got upset, and had jewels of compassion in him. The only thing he didn't do was say all this to me. I just felt it. I thought, "Here's a guy who can take me out of prison even as I remain here. He won't dress me in Buddhist garb, but accept me as I am." I knew he was a tough character.

Questions

1. If someone named Melody had not gone to the trouble to take the next, small step by sending Jarvis some meditation and spiritual books during his trial, is it as likely he would have undergone the transformation that he did? Is the same true for all of us?

2. Mother Teresa once said she liked the "small way" of doing things, not the big way. Can you think of any small acts of kindness that have made a big difference in your life at one time or another?

3. What do you think Jarvis meant by "compassionate ferociousness"? What is the difference between ferociousness and compassionate ferociousness? One might say that many in politics and much of the public have a "ferocious" attitude toward offenders and prisons, but "compassionate ferociousness"? Perhaps one attitude, whether offender, politician or the public is about "giving pain" and the other is about "giving truth."

San Quentin Is Really Rockin' 'n Rollin'

San Quentin is really rockin' 'n' rollin' with violence these days. The scheduled execution date of another death row inmate is the chief external reason for it; the internal reason for some, I think, is that we are not finding ways of keeping our release valves open to let out the feelings closing us in.

One guy described it to me by saying, "Last week the ceiling stood five feet above me. Then three days ago it was only one foot, and just last night I got a fucked-up cramp in my neck from trying to sleep on my right side because the goddamn ceiling felt so close to my face that I couldn't switch over to the other side."

We were on the prison yard together. When I suggested that he meditate with me sometime, he just laughed and walked away.

It is so difficult to integrate my meditation practice with all the suffering here. In trying to live a life that reflects the Buddha's ways, I fail continuously! I know so little! I'm just hanging in there with my meditation. Practice is my best companion.

Questions

1. When we are in pain or around a lot of suffering, it can be very difficult, as Jarvis expressed, to remain clear and calm. Why would this be especially true in an environment such as San Quentin?

2. Why does Jarvis say, "Practice is my best companion"? Why might such practices as meditation, prayer, or reflection be important whether we are in or out of prison?

Angry Faces

"Man, Jarvis. Are you watching the news?" my new neighbor asked from the next cell one evening. I was relaxing, reading a book about meditation.

"I have it on, Omar, but I'm not really watching it," I answered, glancing up at my television. "Why, what's up?"

"Ah, man! Check out Channel Seven. They showing a Ku Klux Klan rally in Louisiana. Man, just look at all those Klansmen screaming and shouting all that white supremacy garbage. Get this: all these idiots is talking about how all the Jews and Blacks is destroying this country. Did you hear what they were saying?"

"Nah, man. I missed it. I have the volume turned down. I'm just using the light to read by. I did see a bunch of angry faces and racist posters, though."

"Oh, OK," said Omar. "Man, I apologize. I didn't mean to take you away from your reading."

"Hey, that's OK. I don't min' you calling over to me about something big in the news. If you see something interesting, let me know."

"Right, right on! I can do that," said Omar, ending our conversation.

About 10 minutes later, Omar hollered, "Hey, Jarvis! Man, check out all those people. It must be a thousand folks marching in San Francisco. Do you see them?"

"Wow!" I said, looking up at the huge demonstration on my screen. "What's up with them?"

"Man, it's an environmentalist demonstration. They demanding an end to the cutting of trees in some places, and all the senseless slaughter of wildlife animals. They saying the planet is being destroyed and more and more kinds of animals is near extinction."

"Is that right? I can tell just by looking that they're upset. You see that one woman raging into the microphone and those demonstrators holding up posters and shouting and getting arrested? Hey, they all must be pretty pissed to be screaming like that and risking going to jail."

A little later Omar yelled, "Hey, check that out. Are you still watching? Look at the president and all those congressmen, right there on national TV, fighting and arguing, each trying to convince the public that the other is at fault for this terrible economy."

"Yeah, I see them. Is that what they're fussing about? I can tell they're in an uproar about something. That one senator, man, he's almost spitting. But you know what's really interesting, Omar?"

"No, what's that?"

"Well, for the first time, I'm starting to see something – that the anger and bitterness on the faces of these congressmen and the president of the United States is the same as on the faces of all those environmentalists and the Klansmen. The only difference is that the Klansmen wore khaki and hoods, the demonstrators were dressed for going to jail, while the congressmen and the president wore real expensive suits."

"I never seen it like that," said Omar. "I get mad when I see the Klan on TV or when I see all what's goin' down. But I never thought until now, Jarvis, that we all wear the same hateful expression."

"Yeah, isn't it a trip?" I said. "But it's something to think about – learning to see everyone's suffering, not just the frustration of those we agree with. Otherwise, let's be honest, all we really want to do is kick a few Klansmen's asses."

"Ah, man . . . man . . . man!" Omar groaned. "I don't think I'll be able to do that. That there is a little too much chile on my hot dog for me."

Questions

1. How do Omar's observations concerning the KKK, the environmentalist demonstration, and the president and legislators demonstrate a sense of connectedness? Can different vocations, levels of education, races, and ideologies mask similarities in our feelings and emotions? Do all people experience suffering?

2. Can a hard and angry heart reside in a corporate executive or college professor as easily as it does in an inmate serving a life sentence in San Quentin?

3. Is the same observation true for a "loving heart?" Do we sometimes not see or experience compassion because of stereotypes we have about certain types of persons? Could a prisoner serving a life sentence in a maximum security prison have a loving heart and influence his or her world in a positive way?

Peace Activist

When I awoke in the early morning to begin my meditation practice, I tried to envision myself as a peace activist in the rough neighborhood of my prison tier. The night before, the once-empty cell adjacent to mine had been filled with the raging of a new inmate. Although his loud voice had filtered into my deep sleep, I refused, as I did every night, to awaken, to lose that very comfortable place that finally made sleeping on a hard concrete prison floor easy.

Now, in the light of dawn appearing in the window opposite my cell, I quietly placed my folded blanket on the cold floor. My new neighbor began to scream again, "I kill you . . . I kill you all, you damn sons a bitches, if y'all don't let me out of here!"

I could see in my mind his hands shaking and rattling his cell bars. I wondered if I could be just as determined to sit in meditation as I had been to sleep through this thunder of human rage reverberating throughout the housing unit. My teacher, Rinpoche, had once sent me a transcript of one of his teachings, where he mentioned a kind of joy that he felt while meditating at airports, waiting for the flights on his busy schedule.

I wished I could remember why he liked this! I decided the answer could be found in something else Rinpoche had said: that there was no time to lose in practicing meditation. I was eager to try this kind of meditation. I could usually meditate within ear range of lots of noise, but nothing as loud and close as my neighbor's steel bars vibrating like a jumbo jet breaking through the skies.

I was only minutes into my practice when my neighbor called over to me. "Hey, dude in the next cell. Save me half of that damn cigarette."

Huh? I thought, my mantra interrupted. I hadn't smoked in years. I imagined someone asking Rinpoche a question like that while he was sitting at the airport. No, they wouldn't dare! I chuckled silently.

I could smell someone smoking in one of the cells not far from mine. I had become accustomed to the smoking habits of my fellow prisoners. On my best days I simply accepted the morning scent as my prison brand of incense. With each lit cigarette, the atmosphere became a smoky shrine for my meditation.

When the wall between my neighbor and I started to move as if an earthquake had hit, I was half tempted to ask him to knock off the banging and join me in meditation. But he would have taken it as an insult, which would only have made me a target for his rage, and his mission in life to make our adjacent living situation pure misery for us both. So I tried to quiet my mind, still sitting on my blanket, still wanting to meditate.

"Hey, dude in the next cell," my neighbor shouted again, pounding on the wall. "Let me have a few tokes of that cigarette. Man, I know you smokin' over there. I know you hear me, man!" He kept shouting and banging.

"Hey, hey!" I yelled. I'd finally had enough and by now was totally convinced I was no Rinpoche. "Man! You don't need to shout and go on beating the wall like a damn fool!" I stepped up to my cell bars. "Man, whatever your name is, that is not me smoking. I don't smoke. I haven't smoked in years. And even if I did smoke, check: the way you've been shouting and beating on that poor wall all morning – which, mind you, has been tryin' to mind its own business, just like me, man – I wouldn't give you jack shit, OK?"

"Ah, man." My neighbor tried to calm his voice. "They call me Bosshog. And all I want is a damn smoke, you know?"

"Well, I'm Jarvis," I replied, "and all I want is my freedom. Believe me, Bosshog, this is not to say that I want it more than you want a cigarette right about now, because I know what cigarettes can make you feel. But by beating on the wall, you're taking what little freedom I have away from me, and that ain't cool, you know?"

"OK, but do you think you can find me a cigarette?" my neighbor pleaded. "I swear to God, man, I've been needing a cigarette all morning, like poor folk in hell need ice water!"

I laughed. I liked the way Bosshog put it – that only poor people needed ice water in hell. As for a cigarette, I always kept extra things for inmates like Bosshog. I would collect old magazines and novels and purchase inexpensive soap and toothpaste and cheap smoking tobacco. I had vowed to do this 15 years back, when I arrived at San Quentin and had to use kitchen butter from my breakfast tray on my badly chapped skin because I had no money to buy lotion from the prison commissary.

"Yeah, I think I can find you a bit of tobacco and some rolling papers," I told him. I sensed from my many years of having neighbors of all sorts that he was one of so many youngsters flooding the prison system for smoking crack or violating their parole.

"But you have to stay cool and not go disturbing the peace on the tier again," I added. "Will you give me your word?"

There was a long silence. To me, this meant Bosshog was taking his word seriously. This made him a rare bird: few new prisoners took even a second before saying anything for a free cigarette.

"Yeah, man," he finally answered. "You drive a hard bargain, but you got a deal! I'll keep it all on cool, my word, man."

"OK, give me a minute." I walked to the back of my cell and rummaged in the box underneath my bunk. I found more than half of a six-ounce can of tobacco left. I had no intention of giving it all to Boss. It was likely that other newcomers would need some, too. Also, the length of time it had taken Boss to decide to accept our agreement probably meant that it would be a struggle for him to keep his end of the bargain. By rationing the tobacco I would keep him at bay.

I looked around my cell for something to wrap the tobacco in. I had a photocopy of Thich Nhat Han's book *Being Peace* that a friend had mailed me. Later, a paperback copy of the book itself had been sent to me from a bookstore, so I reckoned it wouldn't hurt to wrap the tobacco in one of the photocopy pages. And besides, I thought, Thich Nhat Han might appeal to the Bosshog, one page at a time.

"Hey, Boss, do you have a fishline over there?"

"I found one under the bunk," he answered. "Your last neighbor must have left it."

He quickly threw the fishline in front of my cell. I retrieved it, using my own, then tied on the tobacco rolled in paper and watched Boss pull it in.

"Man, right on! Righteous!" he exclaimed happily. "I really appreciate all this smoke!"

"No problem. Perhaps I can send you more in a day or so, you know?"

The bright sun shining through the window told me there wasn't much of the morning left to sit in meditation, but it also ushered in a quiet feeling of having done something as a simple kind of peace activist. Boss had stayed quiet, and the other prisoners hadn't said a word against him moving into our neighborhood.

Over the next months, I kept on sending Boss a daily supply of tobacco, always wrapped in a page of *Being Peace*. Boss was still a bit off his rocker, but I began to consider him a kind of brother. One page at a time he came to like Thich Nhat Han. Every now and then, Boss even tried his best to meditate, but he was never able to stay awake early in the morning, as he put it, "to go on some ol' meditation trip with you, Jay."

After 18 months, Bosshog was released from the grip of San Quentin and from dependence on me for tobacco and *Being Peace*. Before he walked off the tier, he stood in front of my cell and together we recited what had become Boss's mantra – something he'd learned to say whenever he was about to blow his top. We always started off chanting in unison with the words "Man, man," and then, "If we are peaceful, if we are happy, we can smile, and everyone in our family, our entire society will benefit from our peace."

Questions

1. How did Jarvis prepare himself to react to "Bosshog" in a peaceful rather than irritated way?

2. How did humor, practice, and resources (e.g., extra tobacco) contribute to his reaction and the cultivation of his relation with "Bosshog"? What was the significance of the mantra Jarvis had taught "Bosshog"? How did it help him "correct" himself?

Stop! A Buddhist Is Here!

We had been out on the exercise yard for an hour when I noticed a new prisoner approaching the yard gate, looking like a woman. I couldn't believe it. No San Quentin exercise yard hated homosexuals more than this one. Gays came in second only to informants as candidates for stabbings and killings. I knew this was some kind of mistake, or a dirty ploy by the prison administration to get someone killed. Wondering which of these two evils it could be, I glanced up at the tower gunmen.

I'd personally never held anything against homosexuals, but I knew how many of these prisoners felt about them. Some hated them just for hate's sake. Fear motivated others – especially those who had arrived at San Quentin in the early 1980s with life sentences or were on death row and had long ago been taken in by the first media reports that AIDS was exclusively a homosexual disease. Later, prison officials told us that other diseases like tuberculosis were being spread throughout the prisons by homosexuals. The men on the yard had come to believe all this.

"This guy isn't going to last one full hour out here!" I thought. I didn't have to turn around to know that there were other prisoners behind me, looking on coldly, pulling prison-made shanks out of their waistbands. I could feel it. There was silence everywhere. I wanted so badly to holler out and warn this stupid person, "Man, this isn't your damn yard. Don't bring your ass out here." But I couldn't do this. I couldn't say anything. It would have been considered snitching. So I swallowed, kept my mouth shut, and prayed.

Then came a loud clinking and whining as the motorized gate was lifted to let this person onto the yard. When the gate clammed shut, my heart dropped. He had just become a walking dead man. I had seen a few others like this throughout my many years of incarceration.

Everyone in the yard, from those on the basketball and handball courts, to the scattered groups over by the pull-up bar, watched in silence as this fragile man with tiny breasts, his hair in a pony tail, Vaseline on his lips, dressed in tight state jeans, began swishing along the yard fence. I looked up again at the gunmen hovering over the exercise yard and saw that they had already gotten in position. They both had their semiautomatic rifles hanging over the gun rail, readying themselves to fire down on the north wall. Obviously, they knew what everybody else did.

According to the laws of prison life, none of this was supposed to be any business of mine. But it was. This time it had to be. For all the life in me, I couldn't look at this gay person, sitting alone against the back wall of the exercise yard, and not see an innocent human being. Yet I could not summon up the courage to become a snitch and risk my own life to warn him off this yard. Why me, anyway? I felt crossed up.

I had to do something. I began walking along the wall. Dammit. Why were things like this happening more often since I had taken my vows? What would all those people outside these walls who call themselves Buddhists tell me to do? Would they say, "Let's all be Buddhists and just put our knives away and smile?"

I made my way around to where the homosexual was sitting. I passed him several times without stopping, so I could get a good look at him. I wanted to find out if he was aware of what was going on, aware that someone was about to stab him. The fool was not! He sat there like a tiny fish in a shark tank. I needed to think fast, because time was running out. I had to get away from this guy, quick.

I spotted Crazy Dan on the opposite side of the exercise yard. He was squatting, surreptitiously cuffing a long shank in the sleeve of his coat. "Damn!" I muttered. My head began to pound as I watched Dan, a good friend of mine, prepare to knife this innocent person. I had known Dan for more than eight years in San Quentin, and I didn't want him to end his own life trying to take someone else's with two ready gunmen watching.

Then my mind went blank. I began walking along the wall, on the opposite side of the yard from Dan. It wasn't until we both turned the corners and faced each other, with the lone gay man sitting quietly against the back wall, that I saw the shank slowly slide down Dan's coat sleeve into his right hand. I quickened my pace to get to the man before he did. I didn't have time to be scared, or even to think. I just knew I had to get there first.

Quickly, I knelt in front of the gay man and asked if he had a spare cigarette. Dan was only six feet away. I looked up and saw him stopped dead, with his right hand hiding behind his leg, gripping the long shank. He was stunned. I could sense the adrenaline coursing through his body. His eyes, like those of a ferocious beast, stared into mine. I'd never seen those eyes before – they were not the eyes of the Dan I knew. For that split second I thought my friend was going to kill me.

Then something happened. Dan blinked hard several times. He must have realized my silent plea. Maybe he remembered the time I'd stood by him when he too had been marked for death. He turned, and calmly walked away.

"Hey, Daddy, did you want this cigarette or what?" the homosexual asked in a female voice, holding one out to me.

"No, I don't smoke."

He looked around, confused.

When I realized what I had just done, I almost choked on my fear. Why had I put my life on the line for somebody I didn't know or hadn't even seen before? "Am I crazy or just plain stupid?" I wondered, looking in the face of this person who was still totally unaware of what had just happened.

I stood up and walked away, knowing that I would take a lot of heat later that day out on the exercise yard. But I figured I could make the case – which I truly believed – that all this had been one big setup, that the prison authorities had been intent on shooting and killing some of us, and that I wasn't about to let anybody that I knew, especially Crazy Dan, get killed by walking into their trap. The truth, which I would leave out, was that I did it for the gay man, too. He meant nothing to me – except that he was as human as the rest of us. He never came back to our yard after that day, but the incident left me with many questions.

Am I alone? Am I the only Buddhist out here? Does this mean that I, the Lone Buddhist Ranger, am expected to try to stop this madness by myself? I imagined myself raising my hand and yelling, "Stop! A Buddhist is here!"

I can't stop it. It isn't stopping. There are stabbings every day in this place. All I have is my spiritual practice. Every morning and night I fold my blanket under me and meditate on the floor of my cell.

Questions

1. Why did Jarvis put his life on the line to save a homosexual inmate he didn't even know? Did he want to do it? Did he have to do it?

2. What is it about prisons that intensify the fear and hatred expressed by the other inmates on the yard?

3. While most of us will never find ourselves in prison, have we ever found ourselves in a situation where someone who seemed "strange or different" was being treated cruelly by persons around us, some of who might even have been our friends? What was our reaction? Did we react out of fear, ignorance, or prejudice and join in the taunting? Or did we go to the one in need and try to make a difference?

Note

Jarvis Jay Masters (1997). *Finding Freedom: Writings from Death Row*. Padma Publishing, Junction City, CA.

We forget that a person can be a person only in community.
— Parker Palmer

To punish and destroy the oppressor is merely to initiate a new cycle of violence and oppression. The only real liberation is that which liberates both the oppressor and the oppressed.
— Thomas Merton

We are family.
— Sister Sledge

Peace is not the absence of war, it is a virtue, a state of mind, a disposition for benevolence, confidence, justice.
— Benedict Spinoza
1670

Chapter 8

Toward Restorative and Community Justice

Peacemaking criminology has the potential to be effective at many levels. We have already discussed how personal transformation and institutional change can be envisioned by peacemaking criminology. While each of these levels of change are important, there is another opportunity to implement peacemaking that is rapidly gaining momentum around the world as an effective and humane way to deal with offenders. Community justice is emerging as an alternative to the traditional criminal justice system. While there are many variations of the community justice theme, we will concentrate on a process termed *restorative justice* as a way to demonstrate how positive change can occur outside the criminal justice system.

Community justice as practiced by the restorative justice movement cannot be called a new phenomenon, but rather a return to the days when conflicts were resolved at the level of the family, clan, group, and community. The emphasis of community justice is not on the punishment of the offender, but on the restoring of the relationship between the offender and victim, as well as on maintaining order and social and moral balance in the community. Community justice therefore has a broader mandate than the traditional criminal justice system. It must satisfy the concerns of several constituents and produce a result that is viewed both as just and satisfying. In other words, the limited institutional goals of clearing a court docket or ensuring that an offender is punished are not enough for community justice. A more inclusive and healing result is the goal.

Before we discuss the underlying principles of restorative or community justice, we need to examine why the criminal justice system is so unsatisfying in giving people a sense that crime is being dealt with in an effective manner. At the heart of the dissatisfaction with the criminal justice system are two issues. The first issue of concern is the general feeling that the criminal justice system does not work very well, particularly in reflecting the interests of the victims of crime. When an offender commits a crime against an individual, the state takes the case away from the victim and prosecutes it as its own. In point of fact, the state replaces the victim as an aggrieved party and uses its own values and constraints to decide on a disposition. The Norwegian criminologist Nils Christie argues that the conflict between the offender and victim are property that the state takes away.[1] The offender and victim no longer have the opportunity to resolve the case in a mutually satisfying way, and hope of repairing the relationship is diminished.

A second issue of concern with the traditional criminal justice system is its failure to change the criminal behavior of the offender. The over-reliance on punishment that is the hallmark of the criminal justice system ignores some of society's other important goals.[2] The determination of guilt or innocence and the imposition of a punishment are inherently short-sighted activities. If offenders are consistently embittered by their interaction with the criminal justice system, and the issues that contributed to their deciding to violate the law are not addressed, then we should not be surprised that when they are released from prison that they recidivate. A mean-spirited or apathetic criminal justice system will produce a mean-spirited, former inmate who feels he's got nothing to lose. While it is true that an emphasis on punishment does try to achieve the goals of retribution, deterrence, and incapacitation, viewing of the offender as an enemy rather than a family member or neighbor facilitates a punishment mentality that inevitably becomes a self-fulfilling prophecy. The restorative justice movement seeks to reclaim the offender and repair the relationship with the victim and community. Ultimately, this form of justice can be healthier for all concerned.

Underlying Principles of Restorative Justice

Before we examine the process of restorative justice it is useful to look at the underlying principles. Ron Claassen, from the Center for Peacemaking and Conflict Studies at Fresno Pacific College, lists these principles that will guide our later discussion.[3]

1. Crime is primarily an offense against human relationships, and secondarily a violation of the law (since laws are written to protect public safety and fairness in human relationships).

2. Restorative Justice recognizes that crime (violations of persons and relationships) is wrong and should not occur, and also recognizes that after it does there are dangers and opportunities. The danger is that the community, victim(s), and/or offender emerge from the response further alienated, more damaged, disrespected, disempowered, feeling less safe and less cooperative with society. The opportunity is that injustice is recognized, the equity is restored

(restitution and grace), and the future is clarified so that participants are safer, more respectful, and more empowered and cooperative with each other and society.

3. Restorative Justice is a process to "make things as right as possible" which includes: attending to needs created by the offense such as safety and repair of injuries to relationships and physical damage resulting from the offense; and attending to needs related to the cause of the offense (addictions, lack of social or employment skills or resources, lack of moral or ethical base, etc.).

4. The primary victim(s) of a crime is/are the one(s) most impacted by the offense. The secondary victims are others impacted by the crime and might include family members, friends, witnesses, criminal justice officials, community, etc.

5. As soon as immediate victim, community, and offender safety concerns are satisfied, Restorative Justice views the situation as a teachable moment for the offender; an opportunity to encourage the offender to learn new ways of acting and being in the community.

6. Restorative Justice prefers responding to the crime at the earliest point possible and with the maximum amount of voluntary cooperation and minimum coercion, since healing in relationships and new learning are voluntary and cooperative processes.

7. Restorative Justice prefers that most crimes are handled using a cooperative structure including those impacted by the offense as a community to provide support and accountability. This might include primary and secondary victims and family (or substitutes if they choose not to participate), the offender and family, community representatives, government representatives, faith community representatives, and school representatives, etc.

8. Restorative Justice recognizes that not all offenders will choose to be cooperative. Therefore there is a need for outside authority to make decisions for the offender who is not cooperative. The actions of the authorities and the consequences imposed should be tested by whether they are reasonable, restorative, and respective (for victim(s), offender, and community).

9. Restorative Justice prefers that offenders who pose significant safety risks and are not yet cooperative be placed in settings where the emphasis is on safety, values, ethics, responsibility, accountability, and civility. They should be exposed to the impact of their crime(s) on victims, invited to learn empathy, and offered learning opportunities to become better equipped with skills to be a productive member of society. They should continually be invited (not coerced) to become cooperative with the community and be given the opportunity to demonstrate this in appropriate settings as soon as possible.

10. Restorative Justice requires follow-up and accountability structures utilizing the natural community as much as possible, since keeping agreements is the key to building a trusting community.

11. Restorative Justice recognizes and encourages the role of community institutions, including the religious/faith community, in teaching and establishing the moral and ethical standards which build up the community.

It is easy to see how restorative justice principles encompass the concerns of peacemaking criminology. Additionally, the idea of community justice is emphasized. While some of the issues that are embedded in restorative justice can be addressed by the traditional criminal justice system, it is clear that an alternative philosophy is needed. In other words, the restorative justice, community justice, and peacemaking criminology concepts all require the traditional criminal justice system to focus much more broadly on the welfare of the victim, community, and offender. The limited focus on guilt or innocence and punishment are insufficient to achieve the type of healing result that is part of the community justice model.

Given the underlying principles of restorative justice, it becomes useful to ask some questions about the traditional criminal justice system. How did the criminal justice system get to the point where conflicts are taken away from individuals and made crimes where the state is considered the aggrieved party? Is justice concerned only with the punishment of offenders? Is it dysfunctional for society to keep insisting on more and more punishment when it seems not to be effective? Is there a point where the criminal justice industry begins to advocate policies that are more concerned with narrow vocational and economic interests rather than broader concerns of justice?

The Promise of Community

We all live in communities. By this we mean something beyond living in a physical neighborhood. To live in a community means that the individual is connected by social and economic ties to a group of other individuals. The concept of community can become confusing in postmodern times when one knows someone thousands of miles away through the Internet much better than his/her next-door neighbor. Nevertheless, the person next door has the potential to be a friend or a real pain in the neck, depending on just how well you both fulfill the expectations of being neighbors. Those with whom we share this sense of community are partners in developing a physical and shared world. Whether we personally like our neighbors or not, we alternately cooperate and oppose them in our daily lives. They have a tremendous potential to contribute to our quality of life depending on whether they help in times of need or break into our homes and steal our belongings.

This sense of community is what makes stable society possible. In traditional societies, the community did the work that the criminal justice system does in more complex societies. For example, anthropologist William Ury, a leading scholar on conflict resolution, explains how the Bushmen in Africa use the community to resolve conflicts:

> When a serious problem comes up, everyone sits down, all the men and women, and they talk and talk—and talk. Each person has a chance to have his or her say. This open and inclusive process can take days—until the dispute is literally talked out. The community members work hard to discover what social rules have been broken to produce such discord and what needs to be done to restore social harmony. A *kgotla*, which is what they call their discussion, serves as a kind of people's court except that there is no vote by the jury or verdict by the judge; decisions are made by consensus. Unlike a typical court proceeding where one side wins and one side loses, the goal is a stable solution that both disputants and the community can support. As the group conversation proceeds, a consensus about the appropriate solution gradually crystallizes. After making sure that no opposition or ill will remains, the elders voice this emergent consensus.[4]

It can be argued that the differences between the traditional Bushmen society and modern industrial society are vast and that making any kind of comparison between social institutions is fraught with problems. However, the intent of describing the process the Bushmen use for resolving conflicts is to suggest the adversarial way that is used in our court system is not necessarily something that is part of the natural evolution of social institutions. The intent of demonstrating how the Bushmen settle differences is to argue that for the vast majority of the time we have had human social institutions, cooperation and consensus have been important ingredients of stable societies. The contemporary criminal justice system is a relatively recent method for deciding how conflicts get resolved and, as we have previously stated, the results are not particularly satisfying.

Can the community be effective in resolving conflicts in contemporary society? Ury argues that it can. The same processes that are effective in traditional societies can work today. In looking at the declining juvenile crime rate in Boston, Ury credits the community.

> The key, according to Boston Police Commissioner Paul Evans, was "collaboration." The entire community was mobilized. The police worked closely with teachers and parents to search out kids who had missed school or whose grades had dropped. Local government agencies and businesses provided troubled youth with counseling, educational programs, and after-school jobs. Social workers visited their homes. Ministers and pastors mentored them and offered a substitute family for kids who almost never had two and some-

> times not even one parent at home. Community counselors, often
> ex-gang members, hung out with gang members and taught them
> to handle conflict with talk, not guns.[5]

What is unique about the contemporary attempts to use the community in resolving conflicts is the partnering of the community with the government. It is easy to forget that in the larger context, government officials and community members live in the same neighborhoods. In traditional societies, the community performed the functions of government. Today, the social institutions of government have encroached into many of the arenas of the family and community to the point where the influence of the community has lost much of its relevance. The goal of restorative justice programs is bringing the community back into the conflict-resolution process. This involves looking at criminal acts in a more comprehensive and inclusive way. It expands the scope of focus beyond the conflict between the offender and the government by including the victim, other interested parties such as the families of the victim and the offender, and the community itself.

Restorative justice also measures success in a way that is different from the traditional criminal justice system. Rather than worrying about clearing the court docket with plea bargains that leave all parties unsatisfied or even bitter, or keeping score by the number of years of incarceration meted out to an offender, restorative justice is concerned with the healing of relationships and of reclaiming stability in the community. These are, admittedly, more difficult goals to measure but real social justice is a more complex value than the more limited concerns of the contemporary criminal justice system. Real social justice represents a more long-term, rather than short-term, view, and promises to be longer lasting and less likely to see repeated problems.

Finally, restorative justice in the community is superior to the traditional criminal justice system because of the responsibility it places on the offender. Rather than having something done to him or her, the offender must actively participate in the healing process of the community, the victim, and ultimately him or herself. This healing process might be as simple as an apology to the victim, or it might mean paying restitution to recompense the victim's loss. The offender might be required to perform some type of community service to repay the damage done to public property or the social order. But, most importantly, from a restorative justice perspective, the offender must willingly and actively participate in his or her own healing. This might include traditional treatment methods such as drug and alcohol programs, or it could include having offenders publicly take responsibility for their actions and engage in community education programs designed to prevent others from making the same mistakes.

Forms of Restorative Justice

The idea of restoring the damage done by crime is appealing in theory but requires well-thought-out programs to become effective. Simply putting the offender and the victim in the same room together without some guidance or structure is a recipe for disaster. The unresolved conflict could quickly escalate into harsh words and/or violence. There is a process designed to aid the victim and offender in resolving the conflict to their mutual satisfaction. This process is called Victim-Offender Reconciliation Programs.[6]

Victim-Offender Reconciliation Programs (VORP)

Victim-Offender Reconciliation Programs are designed to bring the victim and offender together to forge a resolution to their problem. With the help of a trained mediator, they take proactive roles in inventing creative options to the traditional criminal justice system sanctions. By empowering the victim and offender to suggest and agree upon solutions to their conflict, the VORP process helps resolve disputes in such a way that the outcomes are long-lasting. Victim-Offender Reconciliation Programs may not be appropriate for many cases, so the voluntary participation of the parties is essential. While the term reconciliation implies that both the victim and offender need to reconcile, many times the victim has no motivation to work toward a middle ground because he/she has done nothing wrong for which to recant. Therefore, the term mediation might be a better description of what happens in these programs.

There are three basic objectives to these programs:

1. To identify the injustice

2. To make things right

3. To consider future actions

In the traditional criminal justice system, it is often the case where the victim and offender never get to hear and understand the other's side. The conversation in the traditional criminal justice system is filtered through the police, prosecutor, defense attorney, and the judge. In this adversarial process, the victim and offender are often driven farther apart by positional bargaining. The VORP process gives them the opportunity to meet face-to-face and explain their injuries, motivations, and concerns. In the process of this mediation they often come to understand, sometimes for the very first time, exactly what the other side was thinking. They ask questions of each other. The victim can put a human face on the loss, and the offender has a chance to show remorse. This step of identifying what the injustice has resulted in is, therefore, useful to the victim who gets to tell his/her story and to the offender who gets to explain his/her actions.

Once the facts of the case are agreed upon, or at the least each side has had an opportunity to gain an understanding of the other side's behavior, the stage is set to develop an outcome that makes things right. For the offender this might include such things as an apology, restitution, return of valuables, or any number of other ways to repair the harm done to the victim. For the victim, the setting right of things may include receiving these reparations from the offender in exchange for forgiveness. In many conflicts, the disputants have ongoing relationships whereby the repair of that relationship is important to repair the harm caused by the crime. Simply becoming financially whole often is not enough to satisfy both parties, especially when they may be related. Forgiveness, if sincere, can be a powerful healer and a profound way to correct an injustice.

Once an agreement has been reached, it is written up and signed by both parties. This then becomes part of the court record and has the impact of a legal document. Depending on the jurisdiction, this agreement can be ratified by the criminal court and any violation can result in the offender having to appear before the judge. Alternatively, this agreement can become the basis for a civil suit by the victim against the offender for failure to comply with the conditions.

The agreement may specify the conditions of future actions that could include a payment schedule for restitution, agreement to enter into a treatment program for drug or alcohol abuse, or a pledge to stay away from the victim. In order to prevent the conflict from recurring, this dimension of agreements for future actions can specify how any ongoing relationship might be monitored by the Victim-Offender Reconciliation Program.

Family Group Conferencing

Family Group Conferencing is an extension of the Victim-Offender Reconciliation Program. It involves not only the victim and the offender, but also other parties including family members, the arresting police officer, representatives from the community and/or the government. A mediator coordinates the conference and allows each to have their chance for input. An outcome is agreed upon that accomplishes several goals. First, it resolves the conflict outside the traditional criminal justice system. Secondly, the victim and offender have a chance to confront each other and have their side of the story heard. Thirdly, there is an opportunity for other affected parties to provide input and express their concerns. And finally, the agreements that are forged strengthen the ties of the parties and ultimately of the community. Family Group Conferencing is a process that began in New Zealand and was adopted in Australia and eventually in the United States. The Family Group Conferencing model is used most extensively in the juvenile court where the concern for the offender's welfare is considered as important as the victim's.[7]

Victim-Offender Panels (VOP)

It is not always feasible or appropriate for the victim and offender to meet and try to work out their conflicts. For example, in the case of rape, the victim may be so traumatized that any contact with the offender would be harmful. Also, there are many instances in which the offender is not known and therefore not available for conferencing or reconciliation. This does not mean, however, that some of the benefits of conflict resolution cannot be employed. In these instances Victim-Offender Panels are useful.[8]

Victim-Offenders Panels allow victims to address offenders who have committed the same types of crimes as the victims have experienced. The victims do not confront the individual who harmed them directly, but rather, they confront an offender who has harmed someone else. The idea behind these panels is to allow the victim to express the nature and depth of harm they have experienced to offenders. The victim, thus, plays an educative role in showing offenders the human damage that their crimes can cause. Offenders get to see that their actions have consequences for others and can reflect on the harm they may have caused to their own victims. The result, hopefully, is that offenders will change their anti-social attitudes and behaviors.

Victim-Offender Panels have been shown to be effective with carefully chosen victims of drunk drivers and with victims of burglary. The exact process that these panels provide may vary, but the idea is to give victims a chance to tell their story and to give offenders an opportunity to see how their crimes impact on other people. Again, there is no chance for reconciliation in Victim-Offender Panels because the victims never meet the actual offender, just someone who has committed the same type of crime.

These three types of restorative justice practices demonstrate a very different philosophy from the traditional criminal justice system. They all aim at helping both the victim and the offender and, to a broader extent, the community. Critics of these practices would point to the consequences for the offender, claiming any reconciliation that the offender agrees to cannot include enough punishment to satisfy the concerns of justice. This myopic view of justice, one concerned with the amount of punishment, is inconsistent with restorative justice principles. For the long-lasting resolution of the conflict, and the ultimate well-being of the community, punishment has proven to be ineffective.

Reintegrative Shaming

How can restorative and community justice programs effect real change in the offender? For many individuals, looking at restorative justice for the first time, the idea that punishment is not paramount is disturbing. It appears to these observers that the offender is "getting away" with the crime when there is not substantial punishment. For those who embrace the restorative

justice concept, however, there is a more powerful process at work than punishment. John Braithwaite contrasts shaming and punishment by calling attention to the symbolic nature of each:[9]

> Shaming is more pregnant with symbolic content than punishment.
> Punishment is a denial of confidence in the morality of the offend-
> er by reducing norm compliance to a crude cost-benefit calcula-
> tion; shaming can be a reaffirmation of the morality of the offend-
> er by expressing personal disappointment that the offender should
> do something so out of character, and, if the shaming is reinte-
> grative, by expressing personal satisfaction in seeing the charac-
> ter of the offender restored. Punishment erects barriers between the
> offender and punisher through transforming the relationship into
> one of power assertion and injury; shaming produces a greater
> interconnectedness between the parties, albeit a painful one, an
> interconnectedness which can produce the repulsion of stigmati-
> zation or the establishment of a potentially more positive rela-
> tionship following reintegration. Punishment is often shameful and
> shaming usually punishes. But whereas punishment gets its sym-
> bolic content only from its denunciatory association with sham-
> ing, shaming is pure symbolic content.

Reintegrative shaming casts a stark and powerful light on the offender
in a way that is both positive and transforming. This type of shaming (as contrasted with disintegrative shaming or stigmatization) is designed to bring
the offender back into the social net of the community. Currently our traditional criminal justice system does little in the way of reintegrative shaming. The way the process now works, it is more likely that the victim feels
more shame than the offender. The trial and sentencing that is supposed to
be what Goffman calls a "successful status degradation ceremony" has
become a spectacle about which many offenders feel little shame. This
lack of shame on the part of the offenders occurs because many offenders
identify with the deviant label. Their offender identity becomes a Master
Status whereby they feel pride and accomplishment from the rejection and
stigmatization of society.

Critics of reintegrative shaming point out that it works best in tight-knit,
homogeneous societies like Japan. Given the individualistic nature of
Western nations like the United States, there is concern that the shaming
would not be reintegrative. Many people in the United States are poorly integrated into society to begin with, so the idea that they can be reintegrated
becomes problematic. There are vast differences between cultures, according to the critics of shaming, and to expect cultural bound bonds that work
in one society to be equally effective in another requires a leap of faith that
many are not willing to make.

Some Recent Developments

Gordon Bazemore and Mara Schiff have edited a volume based upon a recent conference focusing on restorative justice's evolution into a broader context of community justice. Kenneth Polk advocates that restorative justice be expanded into the larger arena of social justice, including shifting our emphasis on delinquent and deviant youth to proactively increasing developmental opportunities for youth in general. He suggests the restorative justice movement is at a crossroads; either expand the idea of restorative justice or allow the movement to become one more innovative social control option for the criminal justice system. Mary Achilles and Howard Zehr propose greater, more active inclusion of victims in the restorative justice process, while David Karp and Lynne Walther describe how community reparative boards in Vermont attempt to implement restorative and reintegrative processes within a community justice context. Barry Stuart describes some guiding principles for designing peacemaking circles in communities including accessibility, flexibility, being holistic as part of the empowerment process, incorporating a spiritual dimension, building consensus and being accountable.[10]

In defense of restorative justice, it is just this lack of tightly knit community that restorative justice is trying to inject into the western style of justice. In our postmodern world, we have lost the sense of togetherness that makes meaningful communities possible. No matter how large our efforts or how many "keep out" signs we have posted in our yards, the reality is that we are connected—we are in this thing called life together. What a person does, good or bad, affects others. Rather than seeing this fragmentation as a reason to dismiss restorative justice, we should see as a challenge. Restorative and community justice principles can facilitate not only the healing of victims and offenders, but also many of the ways institutions interact with individuals in society.

Faith-Based Corrections

One interesting trend in community justice is the reemergence of religion as a legitimate and recognized correctional institution. Pepinsky and Quinney identified religious and humanistic intellectual traditions being influential in the development of peacemaking criminology and in an earlier chapter (Chapter 2) we discussed how a variety of religious and wisdom traditions are important precursors. Faith-based programs can provide a spiritual dimension to the rehabilitation of the offender that is not available from other types of programs. For instance, because of the constitutional separation of church and state, government programs must be careful about imposing a religious component into the treatment plan for offenders.

Government programs are limited in their ability to help victims and offenders with faith issues, but faith-based programs are free to explore such issues if the person desires it. By providing practical assistance and opportunities to discuss spiritual and emotional issues in a supportive context, programs can assist victims and offenders in moving beyond their alienation to greater emotional, physical, and spiritual health. Of course, offenders and victims come from diverse ethnic, religious, and cultural backgrounds. They may have varying cultural assumptions about managing anger, grief, and stress. They may be deeply involved in other religions or may be hostile to religion. Programs offering a spiritual component must be sensitive to this and be able to help the victim or offender gain the most from their own tradition and support network.[11]

Faith-based programs can encourage positive changes in offenders in both community-based and institutional environments. Even in prison—even on death row—faith-based experiences can transform lives. While on death row for almost 13 years, Willie Reddix described an inner peace he had found by referring to it as a "quiet light." Walter Correll, an inmate on death row in Virgina, wrote, "Right now I may be on death row, but with Jesus in my life it's life row." (see Chapters 4, 6, and 7 for other examples).

Community Justice and Peacemaking

The purpose of this chapter is to establish the connection between peacemaking criminology and community and restorative justice. Having a correctional system that accomplishes the goals of changing the offender's antisocial behavior and protecting the community requires something that the traditional criminal justice cannot provide. In fact, as we have previously pointed out, the reliance on punishment does little to change the offender's behavior and, in fact, often results in a community that is further threatened with new victims who are harmed. Something else is required to bridge the need for change in an offender's life and the need for the protection of the community. A bridge of compassion recognizes the harms and fear shared by offenders and victims, but also offers a way back into the community for each as well. Community justice is a context where much restoration can take place.

Questions

1. Describe the two issues concerning the traditional criminal justice system that people find unsatisfactory and thus propose a form of community justice. Are these problems ones that can be fixed within the context of the traditional criminal justice system?

2. Ron Claassen presents some underlying principles of restorative justice. Give a brief summary of these principles. Which of them are at odds with the traditional criminal justice system? Which of these principles do you think is most important for healing individuals and the criminal justice system?

3. Explain how the community is intregal to the idea of restorative justice. Is the way the term community is used in restorative justice the say as our everyday understanding? What would a restorative justice program that is integrated into the community look like?

4. What is reintegrative shaming? Speculate on how this principle might be misused in the criminal justice system. Is reintegrative shaming something that can be adapted to the materialistic culture of the United States?

5. Are faith-based correctional programs likely to be effective within the peacemaking criminology context? How might the issues of separation of church and state be addressed within faith-based correctional programs?

Notes

[1] Christie, Nils (1977). "Conflicts as Property." *The British Journal of Criminology,* 17(1):1-15.

[2] Irwin, John and James Austin (1994). *It's About Time: America's Imprisonment Binge.* Belmont, CA: Wadsworth.

[3] These principles are taken from Ron Claassen's web site (www.fresnp.edu/pacs/rjprinc.html). The content has not been edited and they are printed with permission.

[4] Ury, William (1999). *Getting to Peace: Transforming Conflicts at Home, at Work, and in the World.* New York, NY: Viking. 5.

[5] Ury, ibid. p. 10-11.

[6] Van Ness, Daniel and Karen Heetderks Strong (1997). *Restoring Justice.* Cincinnati, OH: Anderson, p. 69-72.

[7] Van Ness and Strong. ibid. p. 73-74.

[8] Van Ness and Strong. ibid. p. 74-76.

[9] Van Ness and Strong. ibid. p. 117.

[10] Van Ness and Strong. ibid. p. 128.

[11] Bazemore, Gordon and Schiff, Mara (eds.) (2001). *Restorative Community Justice; Repairing Harm and Transforming Communities.* Cincinnati, OH: Anderson Publishing Co.

[12] Arriens, Jan (ed.) (1997). *Welcome to Hell.* Boston, MA: Northeastern University Press, p. 25.

When we speak of restorative justice, we run the risk of saying more than we know. And if we are honest, we must admit that we know more than we live.
– Daniel Van Ness

I aint what I wanna be
I aint what I'm gonna be
but Oh Lord
I aint what I used to be.
– An Unknown Slave

Chapter 9
Epilogue

As we come to the end of this book, let us return to its beginning. We need to remember that we are all in it together – the best of us and the worst of us – the best in us and the worst in us. We need to decide whether we will live our lives from the inside-out or from the outside-in.

Each of us is an individual person. Yet, we are also neighbors with other persons in communities, and work in and contribute to various institutions which represent larger groups. In a larger ecological context, we also exist in an interconnected and interdependent "community of life." Considering this theme within the ecology of justice, there is a choice before us individually and collectively. It is the choice of death or life. Fear, greed, an overreliance on the idea of punishment, cynicism, and the resulting loss of hope represent the choice of death. Humility, compassion, service to others (especially the least among us), sacrifice, and a commitment to the possibility of forgiveness and restoration are the choices life offers.

It seems clear to us that personal transformation is the essential element for genuine peaceful and restorative change to begin to occur. No matter what a community's or institution's intentions and incentives are for creating a more just and peaceful environment, if the persons living and working within those boundaries are bound by fear, greed, and selfishness, the process of justice and reconciliation will not be served; in fact, it will be undermined to the point where corruption will become tradition. Conversely, even in the most oppressive communities and institutions, a single person living his or her life from the inside-out, full of peace and compassion, can offer hope to the oppressed and oppressors. A Bonhoeffer, Gandhi, or King can change the lives of persons and institutions through their service and sacrifice. In giving their lives through service and on some occasions with the ultimate sacrifice of death itself, peacemakers through the ages find that their work of peace and justice continues. The seeds of hope they planted are cultivated and nurtured by others who keep the dream alive – the possibility that peace and justice can become a reality for all.

So what will our choice finally be, death or life? Who knows for certain? Only time will tell. But while we are waiting to see how it all turns out, we want to dedicate the future to . . . "the keeper and the kept, the offender and the victim, the parent and the child, the teacher and the student, and the incarcerator and the liberator that is within each of us."[1]

Questions

1. Choose several persons who spent time in prison and either prior to the imprisonment or after they were incarcerated, demonstrated a strong commitment to peacemaking. There are many possibilities to choose from including persons who engaged in civil disobedience of historical note such as Gandhi or Martin Luther King, Jr., or individuals who committed criminal acts and were transformed after they were incarcerated such as Jarvis Masters. What do the persons you chose have in common? How are they different? How did their lives take different paths to a common point? What are the implications for correctional policy and treatment programs?

2. Examine how humane and progressive corrections innovators such as John Augustus and Alexander Maconochie accomplished their breakthrough programs. Where did their creativity and perseverance come from? What lessons can we take from them for today's correctional challenges?

3. Does peacemaking and restorative justice have any relevance for you wherever you might be in your own life at the moment, in terms of personal and work relationships?

Note

[1]   Lozoff, Bo and Braswell, Michael (1989). *Inner Corrections.* Cincinnati, OH: Anderson Publishing Co.

Index